A Gift For:

....

From:

....

50-SOMETHING

* * * * * Fond and Funny Reflections on Midlife

Bill Gray

50-SOMETHING

Fond and Funny Reflections on Midlife
Bill Gray

Copyright © 2005
Hallmark Licensing, Inc.

Published by Hallmark Books, a division of Hallmark Cards, Inc.,
Kansas City, MO 64141
Visit us on the Web at www.Hallmark.com.

Editor: Jane-Elyse Pryor
Art Director: Mark Cordes
Designer: Kendra Inman
Illustrator: Peter Martin
Production Art: Dan Horton

Printed in the USA
BOK2058

For Aaron and Carolyn

CONTENTS

* * * * *

An Explanation 2

The Last Page of This Book 4

WELL, iT SEEMED COOL AT THE TiME

A Brief History of My Hair 8

Necking 17

10 Memorable Pairs of Pants 22

Turn On, Tune In, Drop Everything 30

Radio Killed the Radio Star 35

JOHN, PAUL, GEORGE, RiNGO, AND ME

Okay, So Maybe Time Isn't Really on My Side 42

Like a Pendulum Do 46

Ticket to Walk 50

Bootsteps of the Gods 55

Happiness is a Warm Room 60

Let Us Now Praise Un-famous Men 65

Plane Thinking 70

TO THE PLACE WHERE I BELONG

Baby, I Can Drive My Car 76

Where My Thought's Escapin' 81

There Are Places I Remember… 85

2-Good 2-Be 4-Gotten 92

All the World's a High School Auditorium Stage 96

Foolish on the Hill 100

On the Battlefield 103

Whiz on Down the Road 107

PROTEST, POLITICS, AND PATRIOTISM: A VISIT TO WASHINGTON, D.C.

I Can See Right Down Your Chimney 112

Love/Hate American Style 115

How I Never Learned to Stop Worrying
    and Love the Bomb 120

Grown to Graveyards, Every One 125

What Bullets Cost 129

Facing the Wall 135

Early Afternoon Delight 140

Six Million Hearts 143

Positively Pennsylvania Avenue 146

OLD HiPPiES NEVER DiE

Boom, Baby, Boom 156

There Is a Time…Turn, Turn, Turn 160

K-9 Du Jour 165

And They Will Know Us by Our Elbows 169

I Fought the Lawn and… 173

Fidgeting on a Hot Stove 177

Store Wars 182

Unidentified Foodlike Objects 186

Bye-Bye, Miscellaneous Pie 189

Let It Ow! Let It Ow! Let It Ow! 194

Rhymes With "Old" 197

Paperback Writer, Sort of 201

Dude, Where's My Flying Car? 207

It's Only Words 212

You Say It's My Birthday 216

And in the End… 224

AN EXPLANATION

Every seven seconds in America another baby boomer turns 50. My seven seconds were up recently.

I believe that the past 50 years have been one of the most interesting half-centuries in our nation's history and that the events of those glorious, tumultuous times have shaped the people turning 50 at the dawn of the new century.

The safe, sedate 1950s shaded our view of childhood, the '60s changed the way we looked at politics and our parents, and the disco years altered the way we saw relationships.

The places we've been and the things we've seen have affected the way we do our jobs, spend our money, love our mates, and raise our kids.

Boomers have grown used to being the largest and most influential age group through all the decades, and now, just when we're beginning to figure things out, we must face the fact that we're no longer in charge.

Bummer.

So I thought it might be interesting to think these things through and to write about them in the months leading up to my 50th birthday. Through the generosity of the Barbara Hall Marshall Award program and Hallmark Cards, I was able to take time away from my job as a greeting card writer to research, to reflect, and to have a little fun. For that last part, especially, I visited three of the places that have important meaning in my own journey through the past 50 years: England, birthplace of the Beatles; Washington, D.C., birthplace of protest, politics, and disillusionment; and Pennsylvania, birthplace of me.

Along the way, I wrote about what was on my mind and in my heart, and I learned a little about what it means to be older than I ever imagined I would be.

I hope you have half as much fun reading these essays as I had writing them. No, actually, I hope you have twice as much fun.

At any rate, some kind of time is guaranteed for all. Whether or not it's splendid is your call.

THE LAST PAGE OF THIS BOOK

Here's what it says on the last page of this book:

So after 50 years, here's what I think I've learned:
1. Most people mean well, so everyone deserves the benefit of the doubt.
2. Love is always worth the effort.
3. Life is good.

WELL, IT SEEMED COOL AT THE TIME

Remembering what really mattered: haircuts, bell-bottoms, gold chains, *Hullaballoo*, and Top 40 radio.

A BRiEF HiSTORY OF MY HAiR

Always, always, it was about the hair.

The first haircut I remember having was a butch cut, which is called a crew cut in other places that aren't Pennsylvania in the 1950s.

There used to be photographic evidence of an earlier haircut, which was sort of a modified Hitler cut. Sharp part, with a stray blunt-cut of bangs tilting off the upper right corner of my forehead. But I don't remember that hairstyle any better than I remember the blonde wispy hair I like to imagine I was born with.

The butch cut was also called a buzz cut. This hairstyle had more aliases than a bagman. I remember it being called a buzz cut because my cousin Buzzy got his nickname from his haircut. On him, it looked perfect. The sides were precisely shaved, with exactly matched whitewalls around the farm-tan ears. The top was just the right length and stood at staunch attention.

Think Ricky Nelson at 15.

My butch cut would stand short for about a minute, then collapse forward onto my forehead.

Think Uncle Charley in *My Three Sons.*

The point of the buzz/crew/butch cut was that it was supposed to look casual, but in actuality it was carefully monitored, regimented, and controlled.

In fine 1950s fashion, there was a place for every hair, and every hair was in its place. It was touted as a bold departure from the shiny, cream-filled hairstyles of our fathers, so shellacked to their heads that nary a hair would budge in a hurricane.

But it wasn't, really.

During the colder months, the butch was abandoned for a side-part style. The sides were still shaved, with the top hunkering close to the scalp everywhere except the front, where a wave of hair swept back. We worked that wave every day with black pocket combs, standing shoulder to skinny shoulder in front of the mirror in the boys' bathroom of our elementary school. When my hair was perfect, I slipped the pocket comb into my back jeans pocket, turned away, and headed for the bathroom door. Always I turned back for a last look, and always I had to take out the comb again to make the wave just a little higher, or a little flatter, or a little rounder. I had a secret girlfriend in those days, and I knew if I could just get that wave right, she'd notice me, and our secret love would no longer be secret.

By the time I got back to class, it had fallen completely.

My hair wasn't made for those times.

One Sunday evening in February of 1964, my family wrapped up in blankets in our chilly living room and watched one of the two channels we could pull in on our black and white TV. Ed Sullivan was on, and he spoke the five words that forever changed my hair.

"Ladies and gentlemen…the Beatles!"

My dad sat on the edge of our worn sofa, smoking a Camel straight-end, and offered his opinion.

"They look like a bunch of girls!"

And I knew what I had to do.

Next morning, safely locked in the bathroom, I lifted my pocket comb with trembling hands and combed the bangs forward.

To say the least, the results were disappointing. I had paid my dollar at the barbershop downtown to get the standard little-boy haircut. Rather than have the nice, straight, just-above-the-eyebrows bangs sported by my new heroes, I saw bangs in a perfect triangle. They were just about long enough to reach my right eyebrow, sure, but then they took a sharp upward jag, reaching almost to the hairline on the left side.

I combed my hair quickly back into the great falling wave.

My parents didn't know it, but that day I began to grow a Beatle cut. It took me several years to get there. At first I was scared to go out in public with bangs. Then, when I sufficiently raised my courage, I was informed by my dad that "No son of mine is gonna go around looking like a girl!"

My argument that I didn't look like a girl, but like a Beatle, fell on "dad" ears.

Slowly, centimeter by centimeter, I wore my father down until, around the end of seventh grade, I was wearing my hair in short bangs that curved sharply to the right on the bottom. It was still shaved on the sides and in the back. Even at that, the other kids in junior high were starting to call me "Beatle," which sounded like music to my still totally visible ears. And I think you know what kind of music I mean.

Still, my father kept his eyes on my hair. He seemed to have a knack for knowing exactly when it was starting to be long enough to look good and on that very day he would say, "Billy, time for a haircut."

The next Saturday would find me running a finger along a crack in the brown leather arm of the barber's chair. My nostrils were flaring at the sickly combination of cigarette smoke and half a dozen hair tonics. As the barber tightened the striped sheet around my neck to catch my falling hopes and dreams, I knew that my happiness lay in three little words.

"Leave the top."

I couldn't say it. Instead, I hated myself for saying "regular haircut, please."

When I finally found the courage to say those three magic words, the barber looked at me with a world-weary sort of disappointment. But he left the top.

"I thought you were gonna get a haircut," my dad said when I got home.

"I did."

And so we sang the same duet of the '60s that was being sung by parents and their children all over the world.

My bangs got longer but refused to turn to the right over my forehead and were in my eyes most of the time. Just as with the butch cut, I always had a vision of how cool my hair looked at any given moment, and when I passed a mirror, I was always surprised to be wrong.

While hippies on the coasts were banding their hair into long ponytails, I remained the only kid in my little town with a genuine Beatle cut. Several other boys had Beatles bangs, especially the ones who could play guitar. But they were all fair-weather freaks. They could wear their bangs when they were around other teens, but once at home, a quick part with a wet comb would turn their coifs back into regular haircuts.

When it became clear that there was more at stake than hair, some of the grown-ups in town decided to take action. Shortly after a couple of kids wore black armbands to school on Vietnam Moratorium Day, we got a new principal. He had one of the last remaining crew cuts. He also had a bullet-sized indentation right in the middle of his forehead. No one dared to ask. His first official act was to send word down from on high: boys with Beatle cuts wouldn't be allowed back in school.

I told my dad I didn't intend to get a haircut. His response was surprising.

"They can't tell my kid to get a haircut. I'll go have a talk with this new principal."

Which he did. Then he came home with the results of the meeting.

"Billy, you're gonna have to get a haircut."

It dawns on me all these years later that my dad, who never had much education, really didn't want me to throw mine away over some hair.

Not surprisingly, I couldn't see that at the time.

The worst was yet to come. I walked into the barbershop—for the first time in quite a while—and started to tell the barber how to cut my hair.

"The new principal's already been here. He left written instructions."

It would be that easy, they all thought, to keep the '60s out of their town.

I was 15 and hadn't cried in years, but when I saw that haircut in my bathroom mirror, I cried.

That was the last haircut I got for a while. Parents grew tired of teachers on their knees measuring miniskirts, and the new principal went to some other school where the kids needed to be saved.

The Beatles and the 1960s fell apart at about the same time. Finally freed of high school and on the road to what I was certain was rock-and-roll stardom, I let my freak flag fly. My hair grew to below my slumping shoulders, and I grew a mustache. A couple of months later, people could tell that I'd grown a mustache.

The '70s peeked around the corner. We limped out of Vietnam. Nixon resigned. Looking like our fathers became less and less attractive.

Suddenly, everybody had long hair. Greasers, bikers, actors, football heroes. Even middle-aged guys started to order the long hairpieces.

Those of us who had let our hair go long originally had done it to be different. Now that every Tom, Dick, and hairy Harry had long hair, we had to find another way.

Hello, shag.

The shag haircut was originally a homemade haircut.

All you had to do was lean forward until your long hair hung straight down. Then you grabbed it all in one fist so you made a top-of-the-head ponytail. Then you took scissors in the other hand and hacked off everything below your fist.

As you stood there with a fistful of disembodied hair, the hair that was still on your head fell to layers of uneven, blunt-cut shag. One side was probably longer than the other. The bangs staggered across your forehead. It stood straight up at the crown of your head. It was, in short, the perfect hippie hairstyle.

Then, the same way disco killed music, disco styles killed the shag. Before you could say "Boogie-Oogie-Oogie," guys were paying 25 bucks for a perfectly layered shag, even on all sides, which would fall sharply back into formation after a strong wind, from nature or a blow dryer.

Eventually enough hair spray was added to the mix so that the hair wouldn't move in the wind in the first place.

It was around this time that I had perfect hair for one day.

I was a young 20-something going for the "Dustin Hoffman as Carl Bernstein" hairstyle—long, with a side part, standing a bit atop the head, flowing down the sides and laying perfectly back to cover the ears, over the collar in back without that annoying flip I always got.

And I came out of the shower one morning, fired up the blow dryer, looked in the mirror, and it was perfect.

I drove with the van window down, and when I got where I was going, I ran a hand back through the hair, and when it fell, it was perfect again.

I was singing folk songs that night at a bar in Washington, D.C. I remember one song, an a cappella version of "Thank God I'm a Country Boy." They were all clapping along, and I was singing like John Denver possessed, and all the while I was thinking, "They're looking at the hair. How could they not look at the hair?"

Next morning I woke up, and my hair was sticking straight out on the side, the part was crooked, and it did the Annette Funicello flip in the back.

I got perms for a while in the 1980s. My hair has always been thin, in spite of the fact that many would say my head has always been fat. I could never get my wimpy hair to hold any sort of style. So when it became acceptable for guys who weren't Judy Garland impersonators to get perms, I went for it. It was great to have hair that actually did something.

Of course, this meant I had to sit for a couple of hours in a hair salon with my hair in curlers and stinky chemical goop all over it. I was the editor of a small-town newspaper in Missouri by then, and I spent those two hours silently praying there wouldn't be a fire so I wouldn't have to run onto Main Street with my hair in curlers, which is not a good look for a man with a full beard.

I didn't want to make the front page of my own newspaper.

In my early 30s by then, I had been sporting some gray hairs for 10 years. Now they were staking claim to my entire head.

My perm phase came to an end when:

A. it occurred to me one day that I looked like a fool doing it; and

B. I noticed that if there were curls on top of my head, my hairs were pulled far enough apart that one could gaze right through them to my pink scalp.

I decided early on that I would never be one of those "next stop: hair weave" types who creatively comb their hair over their bald spots. I could see that those guys who lowered their parts an inch a year until eventually they were parting just above the ear were fooling no one.

Imagine my surprise then when I learned that once a certain number of hairs had bailed out, the hair on top of my head began to naturally part farther down toward my ear. All by itself. Really.

I solved this dilemma in my 40s by getting back to where I once belonged. I am again wearing a buzz cut, except now I don't feel any peer pressure to make the crew stand at attention on the top of my head. Just as well, since many of the crewmembers are AWOL.

Oh, it took a while. The abandonment of the principles of our youth often does. And, even after I decided to stop wearing my hair long, I again had to work up the courage to actually say so to a barber.

I know. They're stylists now. Sorry. To me they'll always be barbers.

So I have now replaced "leave the top" with "clippers with a number four." I figure if nature isn't going to leave the top, how can I ask anyone else to?

For the first time in my life, I don't think about my hair much. It does what it does. The part moves farther down toward my ear. My head sunburns in June. The last few remaining brown hairs seem more and more out of place among the gray.

I have bigger things to think about.

Like that one night when my hair was perfect.

NECKiNG

Like a lot of American guys, I've spent the last 40 years or so seeking one particular thing.

That's right. The perfect item to wear around my neck.

My dad was never a tie kind of guy. He had a couple of ties, leftover from the 1940s, but he didn't wear them when I was a kid. We never had that *My Three Sons* moment in front of the mirror when dad teaches son the difference between the Windsor and the four-in-hand.

For Easter Sunday or the church Christmas program, I wore the clip-on. Technically, I about half-wore the clip-on. With a will of its own, one of the clips would leap out from under my white shirt collar the second I was out of my mother's sight. I remained kidfully unaware of this until I fidgeted just the right way, and the hard plastic stabbed me in the neck.

One of the great things about Cub Scouts was that you didn't have to tie the tie. Just a simple slip of the cheap gold-colored neck ring and—Webelo!—your neckerchief was secure! Plus, you got to look a little like Roy Rogers. Always a nice bonus. Fashions took a while to reach my little farm town. We read about them in teen magazines long before we could get them, even if we went as far as Elmira, which had several streets of stores rather than just one.

It was that way with love beads.

I would have worn them as soon as British rockers started imitating San Francisco rockers who wore them, if only I could have bought them. So in the same way that I would later sew lace on the cuffs of my best white shirt to approximate the Edwardian look, I faked beads. My friend Mickey had a Swinger camera, with the goop tube that you had to rub across the instant black and white picture to fix the image. One of the images he fixed showed me hanging upside-down on a swing set, with my green, plastic beads, made from a kid's play jewelry set, dangling down.

I got my first real set of love beads from my first real set of hippie friends. They came from faraway Sayre, a little Pennsylvania town that crowded the New York state border. One of them had made her own love beads from Job's Tears, which she shellacked and strung on fishing line. I could have done that, of course, had it occurred to me. It was so much easier to just do the hippie thing and hint around about how cool her beads were until she gave them to me.

They were one great set of beads. I had a turtleneck sweater I wore under the army coat I got in a trade for the doughboy jacket I bought from some kid for five bucks. When I wore the tan sweater with the olive jacket and the love beads, my hair curling over the sweater neck in the back, I knew I looked just like Jefferson Airplane.

Best of all, when I wore those beads, adults looked at me and looked away quickly, shaking their heads.

The Troy Free Fair came to town for a week every summer when I was a kid. In addition to the dangerously creaky rides run by dangerously creepy carnies, there were souvenir booths. They had always sold cheap necklaces, which they charged too much for. In past summers, the necklaces had been mostly replicas of German iron crosses, made popular by the bad guys in motorcycle movies. Now they added something else that kids could wear to make their parents angry: peace symbols.

The lead dove's foot symbol had been in the magazines and on the album covers we had been buying for quite a while, but no store I knew of sold them. I snapped one up and wore it continuously.

The peace symbol combined a political statement with a badge of membership in the Fraternity of Hip. It also was a way to impress girls. That was a lot of bang for the buck you would otherwise have spent at the fair on a grease-filled paper cup with French fries floating in it.

It was sometimes difficult to follow the fashion leads of the Beatles. Collarless suits were hard for a seventh-grader to come by. You couldn't buy ties that thin, and anyway, I still couldn't tie them.

Around the Sergeant Pepper era, though, the lads started wearing scarves tied around their necks. This we could do.

For a year or so there, my rock band mates and I wore black vests with brightly colored scarves dangling down like fat mockeries of ties. The look could be described as "hippie cowboy," unless you were an adult, in which case it could be described as idiotic.

An added feature of the scarf was that it could be used as one more gauge of who was and wasn't cool. In the same way that bell-bottoms were uncool if they didn't drag on the ground, scarves were uncool if they were the short, "ascotty," Fred-from-Scooby-Doo kind.

The far-out has a way of coming in over time, and by the 1970s, lots of guys were wearing beads. The look got a little less conspicuous as it became more mainstream. Instead of the two or three strands of swaying beads, it became a single strand of tiny white or colored beads worn close to the person's neck.

It was up to the disco years to bring back the excess. Gauze shirts with the top four buttons undone fairly cried for the two or three strands of silver or gold chains that would soon accompany them.

I hated all things disco, except some of the fashions weren't that bad, and some of the music was bearable, and some girls really did look nice without undergarments. I grudgingly worked a beaded silver chain into my wardrobe of plaid work shirts, jeans, and a corduroy suit coat.

I wore that chain every day for years until one day I looked in the mirror and thought to myself, "man that looks dumb."

I was, by then, back to wearing ties.

As the editor of a small newspaper in a small Missouri town, I was allowed to dress as casually as everybody else in town. No jeans—except the wide ones with cuffs—but no dress shirts and ties either.

Then new management came in. And, as is so typical of new management, it felt the strong need to manage for a while. Our new bosses said all the guys had to start wearing ties again. So it was that I would be in a pasture, trying not to stand in cow manure, interviewing a farmer about his trained jumping mule. I'd be the one in the dress shirt and tie.

I'm sure the mule was impressed.

The day I came for my interview to become a greeting card writer at Hallmark, I wore a three-piece vested suit, with a tie. Writers and artists at Hallmark tend to be a casual crew, and I stood out like a geek whose mom dressed him for his first day of school.

*　*　*　*　*

I stopped wearing any kind of beads or chains long ago. Recently, though, I've taken to telling my son about what I think are the good old days, which, I imagine, he thinks are the boring old days.

So I told him about the great set of love beads I used to have.

A few days later, he came back from a trip to the craft store with his mom, who is one crafty lady. He was wearing that wide-open grin that is usually a clue that he has some surprise for his old man.

"Here, Dad."

He held out a thin chain of bright, multicolored metal beads. He was wearing one just like it.

I clasped the chain around my neck.

It's still there.

10 MEMORABLE PAİRS OF PANTS

1. DOUBLE-KNEE JEANS, 1959: Apparently, in addition to being short, having a Ringo-sized nose, and wearing a face that is not quite symmetrical, I have another physical cross to bear: My knees are too high.

When I was in elementary school, my jeans were expected to last the school year. This expectation meant nothing to my knees, which kept on making holes in the front of the jeans whenever I dropped and slid during an especially spirited game of "girls catch the boys."

My mom, ever on the lookout to save money and avoid having to use upper-body strength to push a needle through denim, bought me a pair of double-knee jeans.

My knees refused to get out of joint over this. Instead, they came through the fabric just above the patch that had been glued to the inside of the pants legs to make the double knee.

After that, the double knees were mostly good for making it appear that I was smuggling cardboard beer coasters in my pants.

2. YELLOW CHECKED SLACKS, 1966: Desperate to appear mod, I purchased a pair of pants with small, windowpane checks all over them. In yellow.

They looked very cool, even though they were a bit snug.

They were just barely wider around the cuff than my side-zipper Beatles boots, which meant I was constantly bending down to place the pants over the boots where they belonged. That Sheriff Taylor "pants tucked inside the boots" look was not for the "in" crowd, which I hoped I was in with.

The pants remained a bit snug until they were laundered, which caused them to shrink a size and a half. Defying all laws of physics, the pants actually became tighter than my skin. It was difficult to follow the junior high edict that shirts must always be tucked in. There wasn't enough waist room.

My parents had grown used to the fact that they had birthed a weird kid by that time, but these pants were one look over the line.

"Hey, Mom, where are my yellow checked pants?"

"Gee, Billy, I haven't seen them."

It was up to my brother to tell me the sad truth.

"Dad took them out to the trash barrel last night after you went to bed and burned them."

3. CORDUROY BELL-BOTTOMS, 1967: Bell-bottoms became fashionable long before it was possible to buy them at any store within driving distance. I wanted a pair, of course, and my salvation came in the form of a guy named Jim, who transferred to my little town's junior high from the mysterious big city.

Jim had long red hair, parted close to the center. So I liked him right off. He also had a great pair of royal blue corduroy bell-bottoms.

Jim had a lot of cool clothes and, apparently, the money to buy more. He would grow tired of some of them and sell them to me. He sold me a World War I-style doughboy jacket with a stand-up collar and brass buttons. I wore it to school my first day of 10th grade, even though the coat was made of thick wool and the temperature was in the 80s.

But before that, he sold me the blue bell-bottoms. I was considering using that five-dollar bill to buy the Moby Grape album, but the blue bells seemed a wiser investment. And that was in spite of the fact that the album came with a big poster where one of the band members had managed to sneak an extended middle finger past the photographer.

I fairly glided down the halls with the pants on the next day, and when a friend of mine saw me, he said, "You're kidding, Gray…bell-bottoms?"

My choice was validated.

One warm day after school I was riding my bike, wearing my new blue bell-bottoms and feeling like the banana seat was actually the top of the world. I felt a tug on the right leg of the pants, then heard a jagged, cruel ripping sound.

The flared leg of the pants had caught in the bike chain, ripped straight up, then sharply across, like the corner of an album cover.

For the rest of the summer I had a pair of five-dollar, royal blue corduroy cutoffs to wear swimming. And no Moby Grape album.

4. STRIPED PANTS, 1968: The ironies of life can sometimes be a big pain in the yin-yang.

I had been envying the really good local garage bands for a couple of years when I finally got asked to be in one. Of course, this had to come immediately after the new warden took charge of my high school. To keep from being kicked out, I had traded in my hard-earned Beatle hairstyle for a cut that was the only thing about me that resembled a Marine.

I would have to find some other way to be cool at the first gig with the new band, and I would have to find it yesterday.

Big-city Jim came to the rescue again. Turns out he had purchased my recently injured bell-bottoms from a catalog.

From the same wish book, I ordered a pair of pale blue jeans, with inch-wide rust vertical stripes. The thin, muscular model in the catalog looked magnetic in them, and I assumed I would as well.

I dressed for the performance at the guitarist's house, and when I made my entrance down the stairs wearing the pants, and a purple satin shirt with ruffled cuffs that I had also ordered, I could tell everyone was impressed. Or stunned. Or something.

5. PERFECT JEANS, 1968: Fortunately, stores where I lived began stocking bell-bottom jeans. Unfortunately, they were the Sonny and Cher kind, straight to about mid-ankle, then flared sharply at the bottom. They were better, but they weren't quite hip.

From my friend Truman, who was cool as a snow cone and knew these things, I learned where to get the right kind.

The legs on the pair I got were tight to the knees, then began a slow flaring triangle that widened 'til they dragged on the floor, making only the toes of my shoes visible.

These pants existed long, long ago, before the days of stonewashed or prewashed or acid-washed jeans. Blue jeans would start dark blue in those days, then fade incrementally over time and washings until, one day, you would put them on, and they would be perfect.

Those bells reached that stage, then just kept getting better. I wore them until they fell apart.

6. GRADUATION PANTS, 1970: I was a jeans and corduroy guy. Dress pants were for straights, which meant something else in those days.

So when high school graduation time finally crawled around, my mom had to buy me a pair of dress pants. They were black, with creases so sharp I could have shaved with them, the one day a week I had to shave.

They were 29/32s, snug around the waist, and plenty long enough to wear with the stacked-heel suede cowboy boots I wore to my commencement.

I kept those pants for 10 years after graduation and never wore them. Once a year I took them out of the closet and tried them on to see if they still fit. One year they didn't. That's the year I finally gave them away.

7. PATCHED STRAIGHT LEGS, 1973: I don't know quite when it started. Some rock star, I suppose, showed up with a patch on his blue jeans. Pretty soon everybody who wasn't nobody started patching his or her jeans until it became a contest to see who would have the most interesting patches.

The rules were simple: You could patch with anything except blue denim.

My straight legs actually did wear through in a knee, so I patched it. That was cool, so I patched the other knee because it looked like it might wear through soon. After that I became a patcher without a cause. Red squares, green circles, plaid material from an old work shirt, corduroy, burlap, flannel.

I covered the hole in the back, where the corner of the pocket tore off, with a peace symbol. The long, thin, "U.S. Army" iron-on from an army shirt worked fine for the inside seam. An

American flag went behind the hole in the crotch so the stripes showed through the frayed fabric.

I was actually relieved to finally throw those pants away. Sewing is hard. I could see why my mom went with the double knees.

8. WHITE PLEATED WALKING SHORTS, 1980: I didn't wear shorts in the 1960s. We wore long jeans in the hottest weather. We didn't mind being hot, as long as we were cool.

The old jeans we had cut off were saved primarily for swimming. Even then we would, often as not, just swim in our jeans and then walk them dry again.

So it was quite a lifestyle-changing experience for me to wear the white pleated walking shorts.

It was right after I got engaged, and I really wanted to impress my future in-laws. I figured the shorts oughta do it. Just in case, I also shaved off the straggly beard and traded in my round-rimmed Lennon glasses for a pair of grown-up frames.

It's twenty-some years later, and I'm still married to their daughter.

Some guys slay two-headed, fire-breathing dragons for love. I change my pants.

9. DOCKERS, 1983: I don't know. The date is hazy. It was sometime around '83, I think.

It had been jeans—blue or black—for me since, well, forever. When I needed to get dressed up, I wore corduroy. Except for graduations, funerals, and my wedding, that was as far as I went toward the dark side.

Pleated, cuffed khakis had always been around, but to middle-aged hippies like I was, they were out of the question. Weak tea, I thought. Chess club. College fraternities. The Lettermen. Neither fish nor fowl. You think you're cool in those things just because they're not actually, technically, dress pants. Right? Think again, nerd-o.

So it came as quite a little shock to me when I tried a pair on and caught myself thinking that they looked pretty good. And felt even better.

I had met the enemy and was wearing his pants.

Of course, I wear pleated, cuffed khaki pants quite often these days. Now that guys my age have made them cool.

10. CORDUROY PAINTER'S PANTS, 2001: I buy most of my clothes on the cheap now, cruising the sale racks like a tiger shark through a school of tuna.

Fashion has become less of an issue to me, for one thing. And since I can clearly remember when you could buy jeans and get change from a ten, I recoil at 60-dollar pants. The sight of a guy my age recoiling is not pretty.

I was looking through the 70-percent-off rack when I spotted two pairs of corduroy painter's pants, one tan and one olive. They were both in my size, which is to say loose around the middle and just a little too long. I am still paranoid of unloading the dryer to find I am the owner of flood pants.

My interest was piqued. I still like corduroy and have fond memories of slouching through the 1970s in bone painter's pants. I even had a pair of the bib overall painter's pants for a brief time, but the straps kept sliding off my round shoulders like a Veronica Lake gown.

I held them at arm's length for a long while, these fancy britches that looked like work pants, but would never feel the worn leather of a tool belt.

These were young-guy pants. No doubt about that.

I put them back.

I took them off the rack again.

I put them back again.

Finally, I bought them.

I know that they were already out of style when I bought them, or they wouldn't have been 70 percent off. I know I look a little goofy, swoosh-swoosh-swooshing around with the baggy legs flapping and bunching up on my shoes.

They remind me of my youth.

You want better than that from a pair of pants?

TURN ON, TUNE iN, DROP EVERYTHiNG

Much has been made of the fact that mine is the first generation to have grown up with TV. Psychologists, preachers, principals, and probably some other p-words, have told us how we're all being sucked into a cesspool of moral ruination at warp speed by the unholy eye in the living room. It's the devil in living color, they say. It's chewing gum for the mind. It's a waste of time.

Ahhh, so's yer old man.

Look at me. I've been watching TV my whole life, and I'm perfectly norm…well, OK, bad example.

I suppose there was no TV in my house when I was born in 1952, but there was one there as far back as I can remember. One of my favorite childhood memories, in fact, is coming home from school, grabbing a fistful of Hydrox cookies and a glass of milk for dunkin', then falling to the linoleum in front of *Roy Rogers.*

To my way of thinking, Roy and Dale and Gabby were at least as educational as school was. From Roy I learned always to shoot to wing, never to kill. From Gabby I learned the value of good dental hygiene. And who knew there were Jeeps in the "old West"?

We've all been entertained by television. But even beyond that, TV has given us something to talk about. And as anyone who's ever been to a company picnic knows, that's a valuable gift.

In my life there has been a long line of "shows we all talked about." First, on the school bus or around the lockers; later, in bars and college commons; then at work or in the carpool or while we sat with other parents watching our kids on the jungle gym.

Someday, if I don't face early cancellation from that great programmer in the sky, I expect to be discussing TV shows down at the senior center.

Because my friends and I were rock and rollers in junior high, we always compared notes on the latest installments of *Hullabaloo* and, later, *The Monkees.*

We talked about how cool *Secret Agent* was and then dissected every nuance of Patrick McGoohan's wonderfully weird follow-up, *The Prisoner.*

Slouching around the lathe in wood shop, we talked about Julie Newmar on *Batman,* the way I suppose girls in home ec talked about the hunky guy on *Lost in Space.*

In high school, you bet your bippy we all started saying "Sock it to me!" when *Laugh-In* debuted. And we kept using the show's catch phrases, too, right up to the time teachers started saying them.

Of course, there were others, and there still are shows that affect us like that. More than entertainment, they tint our culture, enter our vocabularies, change the way we dress or wear our hair.

Admit it. You wore the suit coat over the T-shirt. You asked the stylist to cut your hair like Farrah's. You lusted after Michael's leather bomber jacket. OK, maybe that last one was just me.

Don't have a cow about it, man.

I have great memories of communal TV shows, the ones that

seemingly had to be watched with friends.

My two best friends and I used to gather at one of their houses to watch *The Beatles Cartoon* on Saturday mornings, even though we knew it wasn't really their voices. The show used the real songs and had the word "Beatles" in the title. That was enough.

At a college dorm, in the days before every kid had a TV in his or her room, we all gathered to watch *The Night Gallery* episode where Richard Thomas has to eat food off a dead man's chest to absolve the deceased of his sins.

In the Olive Branch Mission, in Chicago's bowery, one bitter winter night, I sprawled on the floor with a bunch of college volunteers to watch Chevy Chase do the "Weekend Update" on *Saturday Night Live.*

In Washington, D.C., we all gathered to watch *Mary Hartman, Mary Hartman.* Later, we all gathered to watch the man in the iron lung play piano on *Fernwood 2Night.* Later still, we watched Statler and Waldorf trade barbs on *The Muppet Show.*

Several of the writers I work with at Hallmark got together over lunch every day for an entire summer to watch videos of the first 100 episodes of *The X-Files,* in order. Try not dropping your sandwich when the mom rolls out from under the bed on her trundle in the "Home" episode.

When watching TV shows as great as those with friends as great as those, the TV is almost incidental. We entertain each other as much as the show entertains any of us. TV is the fuel that floats our "love boat."

I have to agree, though, that a lot of television over the years has been mindless drivel. That's not necessarily a bad thing. Sometimes after a hard day at life, the spirit prefers nachos to carrot sticks.

But I also know that in the 45 years or so I've been watching TV, there has been at least one show every season that I just can't wait to see.

Sometimes they've been the big hits, like *M*A*S*H* or *Hill Street Blues.* Sometimes they've been the ones that don't last long, like *He and She* or *Sports Night.* But they've always been there, impressing me with great writing and innovative styles.

Indeed, contrary to those who said TV would turn our brains to oatmeal, TV has been berra berra good to me. Turns out, while I was collecting all that TV trivia in the brain drawers where geography and math should have been, I was actually preparing for my future job. I learned more about writing jokes from TV than from any textbook, and I've made good use of lots of TV references in the greeting cards I write. The same is true of every other humor writer at Hallmark.

Of course, like everything else, my viewing habits have changed over the years.

I no longer watch a lot of TV, in spite of what you might hear from some people who shall remain my wife. There have been many evenings in my past when I turned the TV on at 6:30 and turned it off on my way to bed. I don't do that anymore. I mean, that would be almost three hours.

Instead, I usually watch only the shows I can't wait to see. And I usually watch those on tape sometime after they've run. Last season there were three of them, all hour-long dramas.

This is an ironic thing. When I was a kid, we had two channels with "sort of OK" reception. We could just barely make out the very snowy picture on a third channel, but only if one of us was on the roof holding the antenna aloft in the night sky.

Now we have cable, which is to say we are air-breathing mammals in suburbia. I have many channels I never watch. Two sports channels. Not interested in sports. Two hip-hop channels. See: sports. We have cable mostly for the CNN and the clear picture and the cartoons.

But I still love TV. I'm still amazed that it's right there, and I can watch it when I feel like it. TV is an old friend I haven't lost touch with over the years.

I can't wait to see what the next great show will be.

RADiO KiLLED THE RADiO STAR

Usually I just hang up.

It's part of the unspoken agreement I have with people who sell things. I don't go to their place of business and sit around in old sweats watching TV, and they don't try to sell me things when I'm in my house.

Maybe it's not actually an agreement, since they don't know about it.

I'm not a call-screener. There's something inside that compels me to answer every ringing phone. Maybe it's just the legacy of being a telephone repairman's kid. Maybe it's that I'm constantly hopeful and expect every call to bring good news.

I used to be so polite that I wouldn't hang up on one of those recorded sales calls. Over time, though, I've done whatever the opposite of mellowing is. Now I hack them off in mid-sentence. If I'm in a good mood, I'll say, "no, thank you" before I hang up.

But a recent telephone intrusion intrigued me. It was a survey. Now, I'm no babe on the phone. I know that recorded surveys often morph into recorded sales calls.

But this one was about music, so I hung on for a minute.

"Hi. I'm not selling anything," the glad-talker began. Right. And hogs don't eat cupcakes.

The voice continued.

"I'm taking a survey for a local radio station."

As I mentioned, I was intrigued. I have some fairly strong opinions about local radio stations. All radio stations, for that matter. Then the kicker…

"Is there a male between the ages of 15 and 44 that I might speak with?"

I answered the recording.

"No, you flaming Gen-X-hole. You'll have to talk to somebody who knows more about music than you'll ever forget."

The recording tried again.

"Is there a female between the ages of 15 and 44?"

And, the final shovelful on the indignity heap…

"Is there another time when I might reach someone between the ages of 15 and 44?"

Apparently, I don't even rank as a second choice. It's like I was the last one waiting to be chosen for volleyball and they decided to go with a life-size cardboard cutout of Dan August instead.

Just like that, a radio station is through with me. Not even so much as an offer to use their best cologne, as long as I wasn't around in the morning when they woke up.

And they're right. I don't much like radio anymore. I stopped listening about the time they reduced the playlist to the same four songs by the same three artists played over and over. They may even be good songs. I don't care. I know from experience that there are not four good songs, but 40 or 400 or 4,000. I seek them out, and I don't look to radio. It takes me about six months of driving to work five days a week to play through my cassette tape collection, and I am constantly adding to it. Swing. Rock and roll. Bluegrass. World War II songs. Rockabilly. Heavy metal. Just good stuff.

A lot of the music I love has no home on any radio station. It isn't easy enough for easy listening, or jazzy enough for jazz. It isn't one of the half dozen tight-pants hat acts on modern country stations. The oldies stations won't play 'em because they weren't big enough hits.

Radio seems to have no respect for the history of the music it plays.

You can hear "Brown-Eyed Girl" until your face is blue, but if Van Morrison puts out a new album, no radio station is going to play it. You're far more likely to hear an old Creedence tune than a new John Fogerty song. I stopped listening to one young country station the day John Denver died and the DJs made tasteless jokes about it, as though John Denver hadn't played a major role in broadening the audience for the music they play every day.

It makes me a little sad that radio and I have gone our separate ways. We had such good times together.

It was almost a religious experience for me. I'd place the white plastic radio on the kitchen counter and turn the dial off the country station my mom was listening to. The signal might be laced with static, so I would turn the radio one way, then another to strengthen it.

The last few seconds took as long as "MacArthur Park," before the announcer would welcome me to the weekly Top 40. That's right. Forty. Over the next couple of hours, while I should have been out in the sunshine, I would stand in front of that little white box as 40 songs danced out of it. Forty-two, actually, since they threw in a golden oldie and a song to watch out for on next week's survey.

And it was a wonderful mix of styles. The Kinks might be followed by Vic Damone. The temptin' Temptations would give way to Annette Funicello or Noel Harrison or the Lettermen.

Of course, for me, one of the best things about the weekly Top 40 was that it would probably have a Beatles song somewhere on it.

Any telephone survey would have told them they were nuts to program music that way. Any focus group would have gladly told them which artists to never, ever play again.

But you won't convince me that my love for a wide variety of musical styles doesn't come partly from those stewpot Top 40s. In the daylight I listened to local stations, but at night, when the atmosphere cooperated better and stations boosted the signals, I could listen to stations like WKBW in far-off exotic Buffalo. Long after I was supposed to be asleep because tomorrow was a school day, I would prop myself up on my pillow with the radio tilting on my chest and listen to the great Joey Reynolds.

The AM signal was uneven at best, but after much trial and error, I learned that I could boost it by placing the flat of my palm on top of the radio. A completely garbled, untranslatable noise would become music at the touch of my hand. Literally, the music was coming out of the air, through me, and into the radio. I felt like a Pentecostal preacher at a miracle healing service.

In the winter, when I could see my breath in my unheated upstairs bedroom as I sang along, I tried to find ways around taking my hand from under the pile of blankets to make the radio work.

I tried putting a towel on top of the radio, hoping to fool it into thinking it was my hand. Not a chance. I tried a pillow. Nope. I tried a loaf of bread. If radios could sneer, I believe it would have.

Finally my brother suggested I try wearing a mitten.

The radio would not be fooled. To listen to clear music from Buffalo on a winter night, I would have to keep one bare hand atop the radio until it got too cold, then warm that hand and freeze the other for a while.

It was that or static in the rock and roll.

Do I have to tell you which I chose?

In those days, radio was worth it.

'Course, that's not the kind of thing phone surveys want to know.

JOHN, PAUL, GEORGE, RINGO, AND ME

England: Birthplace of the Beatles and land of deep toilets.
Let's visit London and day-trip to Liverpool, shall we, mate?

OK, SO MAYBE TiME iSN'T REALLY ON MY SiDE

Winston Churchill used to only sleep about three hours a night. I think that explains a lot. Like, you know how people are always quoting him? I think he probably talked pretty much nonstop, just to keep from nodding off. So the odds of saying something memorable go way up.

I am not Winston Churchill. I need sleep, and lots of it, bub.

My point is this: Once a body has been around the block as many times as mine has, it gets harder to fool.

I noticed this first on my flight from America to England. Around nine at night, all of the passengers over age 22 or so started to go to sleep. We were finished dining on what they amusingly called chicken. I can only assume they were speaking tongue-in-cheek, which I also think is what I ate. Ba-dump-bump!

I was using my pillow for my lower back, which right there proves I'm no spring chicken. Which is not what I ate. Ba-dump-bump!

I'll stop now.

So I was using my blanket as a pillow and my coat as a blanket. My legs had no place to stretch, of course, so they were jammed in front of me, telling me in short bursts of pain that they needed to stretch out.

To sum up, my butt was asleep, but the rest of me refused to join it.

We headed across the pond toward England and, coincidentally, the sunrise. About the time I finally went to sleep, the sun came streaming through the plane windows, like Old Testament rays through storm clouds. It was eight o'clock in England. Since England is six hours ahead of Kansas City, that meant that back home it was, let's see…THE MIDDLE OF THE STUPID NIGHT!

Passengers began to stretch and scratch discreetly, for the most part, as though they thought it was just another normal morning. The cheery attendants came wheeling the breakfast cart down the plane aisle.

My intestines were having none of it.

"What are you doing? Don't send that airline lard cake and two cups of coffee down here! It's the middle of the night! We're shut down! You think I'm gonna wake up the crew on the peristalsis line just for that?"

There was a time, not so awfully long ago, when two hours of sleep would have been plenty. There were many nights in my youth when two hours of sleep was two hours more than I had time for. Life was all about the adventure, and sleep was a big waste of time. I remember being a little drowsy on the days after I stayed up all night, but never to the point where I considered sacrificing life for bed.

Now I live by patterns and routines. I like sleep. I enjoy being safe and snug in my own bed in my own house, dreaming my pleasant dreams until my wife pokes me in the back to stop me from snoring.

I decided to do what any world traveler—which is what I was pretending to be—is supposed to do—I smiled, although I'm not a morning smiler, and said, "Mornin'," although I'm not a morning talker, and stumbled off the plane, because I am a morning stumbler.

And I determined to beat this time change/jet lag bugaboo. I'm an American, after all! I'm a guy!

I stayed up 'til my normal 9 p.m. bedtime, which meant I had slept about two hours of the past 30 or so, then turned in. Within minutes, Morpheus and I were dancing the horizontal tango. I slept deep and hard. For about two hours.

If you want to know what the ceiling of a London hotel room looks like in the dark, I can tell you. I stared at one most of the night. Around morning, which would have been bedtime back home, I fell asleep again until the alarm went off about two hours later.

After a full day of bleary-eyed Londoning, I got back to my hotel about 6:30, splashed some cold water on my face, and went out to find dinner.

Here's something I didn't know: Most of the pubs and little local restaurants in Britain stop serving dinner around 6:30. They eat dinner at 5, which my stomach knew for a fact was really 11 in the morning. I was out of luck and out of dinner. I wandered, hungry as a clod, until I finally found the one place I could get a sandwich. Starbucks.

Yeah, I know. I could probably have eaten at a Starbucks without flying halfway around the globe. I wouldn't be surprised to find they've put one up in my backyard by the time I get home. And I really didn't want to be one of those Americans who visit another country but will eat only in American fast-food chains. I would have tried the fish and chips! I would have sampled steak and kidney pie! Oh, I wouldn't have liked them, probably, but that's not the point!

OK, SO MAYBE TIME ISN'T REALLY ON MY SIDE

I swallowed my pride and bought a panini. Then I swallowed the panini.

All of you proprietors of little British pubs who live off tourist dollars, all of you Basil Fawltys with your quaint British lodging houses, all of you caffeine-jittered owners of mom-and-pop coffee shops…well, all I can say is, don't blame me, blame my stomach and its steadfast refusal to change routines.

We can discuss it when I wake up.

LiKE A PENDULUM DO

London Bridge isn't falling down after all. I know because I saw it today with my own two feet, or walked across it with my own two eyes. Or something. I'm a little time-change flummoxed.

I learned a few other things today:

•If today's any example, it doesn't always rain in London. But you can never be sure when it's going to rain.

•Every bloke and bird on the street (OK, now I'm just showing off) has a cell phone in his or her coat pocket. For a country about the size of New Hampshire on a water-weight day, these people have a tough time waiting until they get home to talk to each other. It's like every person here is a teenage girl in a mall in Iowa.

•Londoners are usually tolerant and just plain nice to visitors, even Americans who act a little superior while asking directions to someplace that's right across the street.

•A one-pound coin is just the cutest little thing.

I made these discoveries while doing a very old-guy touristy thing. I rode a tour bus that drove 'round and 'round the city, pointing out places of interest. Well, OK, since you asked, the bus didn't actually point out the places of interest. On some of the buses we wore silly looking headphones. On other buses we had a live tour guide. I much preferred the live guy. Not only am I impressed with how well they memorize and present facts, it amazes me that they can repeat the same stuff day after day without just screaming, "Open your eyes, people! It's all right there! You're all big boys and girls! Get off your lazy bums and use your feet! Explore! Discover!"

But they don't. They maintain control. I'm guessing many of them are unemployed actors just filling time until they find jobs as waiters.

They always make me appreciate my job a little more.

I complimented one of our tour guides because he did a really good job. He looked up and said, "What...?" surprised that anyone actually knew he was there. So I repeated the compliment, and he grinned sincerely and said, "Thanks, mate!"

And if you don't think that makes my "high points of the trip" list, well, you're no mate of mine.

When I tell friends—especially my younger friends—about these guided tour things, they are always taken aback. I can tell they think I'm a travel wimp and that I might as well buy the matching white shoes and belt now because I'm already livin' the retiree's dream.

They're the ones who backpacked across Italy that summer between high school and college, and next year they think they'll go to New Zealand.

And in truth, it wasn't that long ago I agreed with them.

I was in San Francisco, I think, the first time I sort of sheepishly signed up for a guided bus tour of the city. I had a heaping helping of second thoughts with dinner. A guided bus tour! Guided bus tours were for old people!

But I loved it. To paraphrase Dylan, I've got a head full of trivia that's drivin' me insane, and I live to cram more useless junk in there. The tour guide offered a litany of factlets, and I inhaled them and stored them to bore friends and co-workers with at a later time.

When I realized that I was having guided fun, I had to re-think my original position. Guided bus tours must be for young people too.

Because if that wasn't the case, then I must be getting…well, you see why I had to reach that conclusion.

So I saw the sights of London from the top deck of a double-decker bus. I wore the silly headphones, and every strong, pint o' bitters-drinkin' London man and every good-looking, mini-skirted London woman who saw me knew me for the helpless tourist I was. I snapped pictures and heard trivia and quite enjoyed myself.

Even though I felt they left a few vital things out.

Not once did the name "Herman's Hermits" come up, for example. Our guide never said anything like, "And that's the street corner where Keith Richards was arrested for public uri-nation." Although Lord knows there must be dozens of them.

Not even so much as "…and that's Albert Hall. Notice the holes."

It appears no one told these people why I came to London in the first place—how my trip here is the fulfillment of a dream that started one February night when I was 11, watching Ed Sullivan.

For a while in the 1960s, there was a television sitcom called *Fair Exchange.* It was about a family in England and a family in America who let their teenage kids change places for a while. I always felt sorry for the poor British kid who had to come to America.

London was the epicenter then, where everything happened. It was where the Beatles were, which, to me, meant it was where the future lived. Everything good and exciting in music and fashion and lifestyle was coming out of England, and I sat in my room on the other side of the planet, playing *Meet the Beatles* over and over, working on my English accent, and dreaming of the day I could visit.

Today, a mere 30-very-odd years later, I made it.

TiCKET TO WALK

OK, it's official. I can no longer make fun of Star Trek nerds.

Today I went on a guided Beatles walk. I traipsed around the side streets of London with a goofy, nirvanic grin on my face, listening as our guide filled us in on the minutiae that only a hopeless Beatles-nerdiac would appreciate.

I loved it.

And might I add, those pointed rubber Vulcan ears look really cool on you, sir.

We were to meet our guide, Richard, at 11:20 at the front of Marylebone Tube Station. Right around 11, a guy, who looked pretty much like you'd expect a guy who leads Beatles walks for a living to look, walked out into the open and held up a brochure that said "London Walks Beatles Walk."

Yes, "London WALKS." The same company that sponsored our walk also offered walks for Sherlock Holmes nerds, royalty nerds, and Jack the Ripper nerds, among others.

Boy, the things some people won't waste their time on.

I didn't want to be the first to approach him out there in the middle of the concourse. This presented a problem, since I figured there would be a good chance I would be the only one approaching him. Oh, I of little faith.

Three others identified themselves first. There were a couple, who looked to be in their early 30s or so, and a young man from

Japan. OK, so it wouldn't just be the guide and I, walking the streets of London.

When there were only a few of us, we were all hesitant to stand too close. I backed off aways and leaned against a mailbox. One couple went off and sat on a bench, watching to make sure the tour didn't leave without them.

People kept coming up, and eventually there were about 50 of us—several couples, a family or two, a group of college-age women, and several touring alone, like I was. We ranged in age from a girl of about 10, there with her father, through high school- and college-age people, to young couples, to older couples, all the way up to, well, me. I may well have been the oldest person on the tour that day, which, to my mind, meant I won. How many of them could clearly remember Ed Sullivan mispronouncing the word "Beatles"?

More than half of the people on the tour were women, by the way, and a bunch of them were women in their 20s. Take that, Trekkies.

Richard, the guide, is known as "the Pied Piper of Beatlemania," which I suppose made all of us rats. He is also known as the "Beatle Brain of Britain."

He is not, however, known as the "Beatle Brain of Shawnee, Kansas," since that's, well, me again.

After he explained to us that the opening scenes for *Hard Day's Night* were filmed in the very station where we were standing in a herd, grinning like ninnies, he led us down, not to a bridge by a fountain, but to the corner.

Two scruffy blokes—yeah, I know, but that's the best word for them—passed through the center of our group and headed for the station door.

"Did you all see that?" he asked conspiratorially. "That was

Noel and Liam Gallagher!"

We all turned and looked, and sure enough, the two brothers from Oasis were disappearing into the station.

He seemed more excited by that than I was. What did I care about a couple of pretenders when I had come to hear about the originals?

Will there be 50 people standing on that corner in 30 years, waiting to hear about where Oasis used to hang out? I think not.

Fortunately, he got back to vital things by pointing out that the narrow side street we were in front of was the one George falls down on at the beginning of *Hard Day's Night*. I took a picture of the street. Then I took another picture of the street, just in case the street had moved in the first picture.

For the next hour we clotted along, past row houses and businesses, stopping and bunching together now and then so Richard could give us the goods.

I was really enjoying the tour, walking the same sidewalks that Beatles' boots once trod. At least I'll bet they're the same. How often do they replace sidewalks? But I was enjoying just as much being in the company of that many other people who loved their memories of the Beatles so much that they were more than willing to be embarrassed in public for them. As the group moved, I would hear them trying to out-Beatle-trivia each other, or they would be sharing memories about their favorite songs.

The Londoners around us trying to get on with a hard day's work probably thought we were silly. And so we were. At one point, person after person took pictures of a black door with the number 57 on it. How many of those are there around, do you suppose? You can probably find doors like that on lots of streets, right between numbers 56 and 58.

But this door used to lead to the Asher home, and it was on the top floor of that home that the Asher daughter Jane's boyfriend, Paul McCartney, wrote "Scrambled eggs…Baby how I love your legs…"

And we pretended not to know that "Scrambled Eggs" was the song that became "Yesterday" because Richard was having such obvious fun telling us.

We ended at Abbey Road in front of the studio where the Beatles recorded their music. Groups of four would walk across the street, trying to re-create the shot from the *Abbey Road* album cover and, to a lesser extent, trying not to get killed by oncoming traffic. Fans do that every day, day after day, and have been for 30 years. We don't forget.

I looked through the gates at the building, which probably looks completely different than it did when the Beatles were recording there. And I remembered something the tour guide told us on the London bus tour the day before.

There was a part of London that was a fish market until they moved it several generations ago. And the people in the office buildings say you can still smell the fish.

Just like I'll bet you can still feel the Beatles in Abbey Road Studio.

I stared through that gate, past the flowers and notes fans were still leaving for George and John, and thought about the songs that came out of that place. How I waited for the next one, to see if it would be as great as the others. How it always was. Or how, on those days when school was too hard and home wasn't any better, a new Beatles song would burst forth just in time to save me. And how much fun it is even now to play those songs again, on my car CD player or in my head.

My folks, like all parents, thought I'd grow out of this Beatles thing.

I never have.

BOOTSTEPS OF THE GODS

I suppose I should explain myself.

I have flown halfway across the United States, all the way across an ocean to London, then taken a two hour and 55 minute train ride north, to sit in a Liverpool hotel room in this jumble of old stone buildings, new shopping malls, and empty stores by the British coast.

All because 45 years ago two boys met at a church hall after a village picnic.

And yes, thank you very much, I'm quite pleased to be here. This is nothing less than a pilgrimage.

It seems silly now to say that the Beatles changed my life. But the silliness doesn't make it any less true. The reason for me could be a reason shared by a lot of people around my age who hold memories of a pop band so close to their souls.

It has to do with a convergence.

I was 11 the first time I heard the Beatles, which meant I was in sixth grade. By September of the same year—1964—the Beatles were one of the biggest pop acts ever. And I was about to start junior high.

For some people, the most formative years of their lives revolve around college, but in small farm towns like mine, it happens in junior high and high school. Those are the six years when you figure out who you want to be, and then figure out if you can. You start junior high as a gelatinous mass, and six years later—if you didn't drop out or join the service—you are solidified.

First love, first lost love, the maturation of your body, the beginnings of your politicization, a questioning of parental authority, the realization that there is a world outside of your little town…they all happened in high school.

And for me, that was 1964 to 1970.

The nation had been kicked in the solar plexus at the end of 1963 when John Kennedy was killed. Then, before we could catch our breath, the man we were told had killed him was also murdered. I saw that happen on TV. I was 11.

Lyndon Johnson sincerely wanted to create a Great Society and was using all of his exceptional political wiles to do it. But, darn the luck, that pesky Vietnam just kept sucking him in deeper and deeper.

Students protested the war. Whites fought to keep the South segregated, and blacks rioted in the streets in reply. Martin Luther King Jr. was killed. Bobby Kennedy followed his brother into Valhalla. The Democrats may have been the party of peace, but they couldn't stop heads from being busted at their own convention in Chicago.

Parents began to lose control of the kids who didn't see why they should be the ones to sacrifice for their parents' politics.

The future meant little to people who assumed nuclear war was inevitable, so "today" became all. Love was free, which made it all the more frustrating when you couldn't find it.

And a whole lot of that happened between 1963 and 1970.

My high school friends and I, of course, had better things to think about. How hot are those cinnamon toothpicks? Can you do "over the falls" with that yo-yo? Goin' roller skatin' Friday night?

But it would be wrong to say we were unaffected, that we didn't share the nation's doubt and insecurity or feel the nibbling fear that the world was a big rowboat drifting toward a minefield and nobody had oars.

So we turned the radio up and danced on the thin ice.

The Beatles took America in 1964, about the time people my age started junior high. They broke up in 1970.

For those half dozen defining years, they were the background music to my generations' coming of age.

There were other musicians around, of course, and they were great, but they weren't the Beatles. You can argue about who's the best rock band recording these days. There was no argument while the Beatles were together. It was simple. There were the Beatles, and then there was everybody else.

Other bands waited to see what the Beatles would do, so they would know the things they should do.

And musicians weren't the only ones.

My friends and I devoured 25-cent magazines about rock music in the '60s, and all the magazines had the Beatles on the covers. I bought Beatle bubble-gum cards and glued plastic model Beatles like other kids made model airplanes. I chose snare drum in my school band because they didn't have electric guitars. My mother could never find her broom because I had it upstairs, pretending it was Paul's bass.

Soon rock bands were breaking out all over the faces of small farm towns like mine. An amazing percentage of my friends played guitar, and we formed bands and broke up and reformed through the '60s, playing for any birthday party or sock hop that would pay us enough for pizza afterward. We played "Louie, Louie" and "House of the Rising Sun" and "Wipeout" and

"Gloria." But, in the beginning at least, we never played Beatle songs. We wouldn't have dared. Besides, by that time they had gone way beyond three guitars and a drum set.

The Beatles broke every rule, because they could. String quartet on this one? Fine. Brass band here? Good idea! Sitar, anyone? Stunning new song followed stunning new song, and in my life I loved them all.

It was up to other bands to follow their leads. "As Tears Go By" came after "Yesterday." "Cry Like a Baby" followed "Norwegian Wood." "Tommy" trailed "Sgt. Pepper."

And it wasn't just music.

The Goldwater conservative, ex-jock, basketball coach/teacher in my junior high had a light blue collarless suit jacket that he wouldn't have had without the Beatles. Because the boys were from England, the world looked to London, and suddenly all fashion was being dictated by one street.

Parents watched in fear as their daughters' skirts got shorter, and their sons' hair got longer. Men who wouldn't have dreamed of it a few years before were wearing wildly flowered ties. The Beatles did nothing less than take on our fathers' sacred edicts of masculinity: that a man's hair must be short, and each of those hairs should remain under his continuous control. Beatle cuts in 1964 were shockingly long and gloriously unruly, and they grew more so with time.

And, not incidentally, it was a fashion trend that couldn't be followed by a lot of men past a certain age. Beatle cuts were for the young because after the Beatles, the young were in charge. Of course, this meant we were in charge long before we knew what we were doing. It was just a short step, then, until we began to look to our lads for our political views as well. It was the time of peace symbols, and "make love, not war," and two-finger peace signs, and "What if they gave a war and nobody came?" and "All You Need Is Love."

And my music-worshipping friends and I, in all of our teenage wisdom, began to think that maybe there really was a way that didn't involve weapons and warfare.

Now 40 years of yesterdays have hurried by, and I haven't forgotten. I can't remember anything I learned in four years of high school Spanish, but I can remember the words to any Beatles song. When I want to know what year some important event took place in my youth, I think of the Beatles song that was popular at the time. I signed the Snoopy birthday card I sent to the first girl I ever kissed "P.S., I Love You." My last computer passcode at work was "28IF." (I won't tell you what my current one is, but it's a Beatles song title too.) The night my son was born I sang "Yellow Submarine" as his lullaby.

All because of four boys from Liverpool.

Ah, Liverpool. It's right there tonight, outside the hotel room window.

And that's why I'm right here.

HAPPiNESS iS A WARM ROOM

"Sit on the left."

I was in the "From Me To You" Beatles shop in the Cavern Walks shopping center, just a few doors down the alley from the Cavern Club. Steve, the owner, had been chatting with me while I looked through T-shirts, trying to find the right one.

I am a very particular Beatles nerd.

See, the thing about Beatles T-shirts is they tend to put big designs on the front, and when they do, part of the design disappears into your jeans when you tuck the shirt in. This I have learned through sad and bitter experience.

I was looking, then, for shirts with the designs in the upper half of the shirt, in my size, that I liked, that didn't cost too much, in the right color, from one of my favorite Beatles eras. I mean, these shirts had to be just right. It's not like I could come back to Liverpool and exchange them. It was taking a while.

"Let me know if you want to take any of those out of the packages to see if they're the right size," Steve was saying.

And I did. And it wasn't. I was trying to shove it back into the sack, when Steve said, "Oh, no…let me do that." And he did.

So I liked Steve's style, and we were talking.

"Got your ticket for the Magical Mystery Tour yet?"

I told him I was going the following day.

"Oh, good. Then you'll have Eddie. He's good. Knows Paul."

Then, he said it.

"Sit on the left."

I perked up.

"The best views are on the left. People on the right always wish they'd sat on the left."

"All right, guy!" I said enthusiastically, having forgotten that he told me moments before that his name was. "Sit on the left! That's what I want to hear! An insider tip!"

While I was paying for my shirts, he said, "Let me give you something." He handed me a flier for a band called the Blue Meanies.

"Best band around," he said. "Playing tomorrow night up on the corner. Great Beatles stuff. This'll get you in free."

The following day I rode the gaily painted Magical Mystery Tour bus through wet and windy Liverpool. Afterward, I went to my hotel room and hammered away on my laptop for a while. When I finished the day's writing, it was about quarter after nine, or 21:15 as they insist on calling it over there. It was a dark, rainy, Twilight-Zoney night in Olde Liverpool. Gazing through my window to the streets below, I saw Liverpudlians straining into the wind. It wasn't bad enough they have to be called something like "Liverpudlians," now they have cold rain to contend with.

I thought about Matthew Street, a 15-minute walk away, and how I really should go. If I was in my 20s or 30s, I'd already have been there.

Then I paced a while.

"Man," I lectured myself, "There are people out there who would hurt you. They'll take your money and leave you bleeding. It's a stupid, silly risk. You've had a great Beatles adventure. Don't blow it now."

And I paced a little more.

"But it's Beatles, man." My internal argument now had two voices.

"No, it's not. It's some punks pretending to be Beatles."

OK. So that was a good point.

I tried to decide not to go. I went to the window and looked out again. There were people out there, and they seemed safe enough. Still…

I thought of the cover story I would use back home.

"Did you hear any Liverpool bands?" people might ask.

"Oh, I could have," I would say. "But it was late and cold and rainy, and I'd had a lot of Beatles experiences already and, well, I just decided against it. Besides, I'm just not a loud, smoky rock bar kinda guy anymore."

That's what I'd say.

I sat on the bed, leaning back against the pillow. Then I addressed the nobody in the room.

"Aw, to heck with it. In for a ha-penny, in for a pound."

And I put on my coat and went for the door.

Liverpool smelled of wet stone and brick as I buried my hands in my pockets and walked into the spitting wind.

Just around the first corner, I passed a group of teenagers on the sidewalk. The boys were tough high school kids, deep in their cups, shouting everything like they were the new kings of Liverpool. The girls were dressed in way too little for such a cold night, and I knew that they had also been fortified with a little something against the chill.

I know from my studies those boys are exactly what John Lennon would have been like at their age.

Of course, I also remember reading that when John was that age, he used to roll drunks for loose change and fight anybody who looked at him wrong.

I got past the young toughs without looking at them wrong and walked down the hill toward a typical English pub. Loud techno music and thick, sharp smoke were coming out the open door. Inside I could see young men and women strutting through mating rituals.

I thought of my days as a bartender and about how nothing impresses girls in a bar like picking a fight with someone. Anyone. Me.

My destination was down a dark street, and I walked it bundled tight in my fake World War II flyer jacket with the American flag patch on the sleeve, the one that fairly screams, "American tourist! American tourist! Probably has lots of cash and credit cards! American tourist!"

The Cavern itself is in an alley, lined with drunks, and people who weren't drunks but were drunk anyway, and the ubiquitous night-people who make their living asking for spare change. I was nervous right up to the moment I walked into the bar.

I should have known better.

I used to live in the innerest part of an inner city, and I head into downtown Kansas City sometimes now. I've been lost in New York, walked barefoot through Harlem, and felt the strange Boston sensation of knowing you have just moved into a completely different ethnic neighborhood in the space of a block. I've walked after dark through the Chinatown section of San Francisco to get to the Italian section for pasta. And I've learned the same lesson over and over.

The vast majority of people aren't out to get you.

If I walk down the street of any city counting hundred dollar bills, I will probably get mugged. But if not, I probably won't.

People are just too busy stayin' alive to be concerned with me.

The fear that we feel of each other after dark is largely the product of our own overactive imaginations.

How many roads do I have to walk down before I know that?

The band was fine. I walked in on "Ticket to Ride" and stayed in the middle of a big crowd of middle-aged tourists singing along through "And Your Bird Can Sing" and "Twist and Shout."

That was enough. I had proved to myself that I could still, by god, go out on the town if I wanted to. I am not too old to go clubbing after all. I've still got it goin' on, or whatever the current phrase is for havin' it goin' on.

But the truth is that I'm actually not a loud, smoky rock bar kinda guy anymore. And I'm cool with that.

Back in my hotel room I congratulated myself on my spirit of adventure. Then I fished my credit cards and American cash from where I'd hidden them just before I left.

LET US NOW PRAiSE UN-FAMOUS MEN

I am not famous.

Right. Like I had to tell you that.

The thing is, I always thought I would be. Now I don't mean that I occasionally had a passing thought that one day I might achieve some measure of notability. Nope. I always believed to my core that I was destined to be enormously famous.

Maybe you felt that way too. Maybe for you it was baseball, as it was for my father when he was young. Maybe it was country and western music, as it was for my mother when she was a girl. Maybe it was ballet or art or politics or being a rodeo cowboy.

For me, it was rock and roll. Music was supposed to make me famous.

It didn't.

This was brought home to me again as I sat in a bus painted just like the one the Beatles used in Magical Mystery Tour. Eddie, our affable and competent tour guide, was pointing out the places where Beatles were born or went to school or met each other. He also told us how his partner and straight man, Les, who drove the bus, was born on the same day in the same hospital as Paul McCartney.

It occurred to me that there is no bus tour past the church in Alba, Pennsylvania, where I played my first rock gig with the Fourth Regiment in 1966; or the old Springfield Elementary

School; or the American Legion Hall in Wellsboro where the Modds used to play on Friday nights when I was their singer.

And being born in the Tyler Memorial Hospital in Meshoppin on June 20, 1952, just doesn't have that much of a cachet.

Because I am not now, and never have been, a famous person.

OK, get ready…here comes the hard part to write: I never will be.

I think there are reasons beyond reason for things. The reason I came to Liverpool was to pay homage to the most important influence of my teenage years.

But I think I may also have come here, now, as I'm about to turn half a century old, to finally realize that fame is not in the hand I was dealt.

I started dreaming of fame when I was 11. I saw girls scream at the Beatles, and knew, like seeing a Jimmy Jet on TV, that I must have that.

One short step in Beatle boots would get me from wanting fame to becoming absolutely certain I'd achieve it. Another short step and I began to think, by age 12 or so, that I already was famous. People just didn't know it yet. But that, I knew, was just a matter of time, and time was on my side.

I knew the Beatles were each about 20 years old. I would be 20 in about eight years. Therefore, I would be world famous in about eight years. Even a complete dolt at arithmetic—which I was—could do that equation.

I didn't have the normal midlife crisis at age 40. I had it at age 20, when my birthday came and went, and I was still unknown. I had certainly been doing my part, as a drummer and a singer in a variety of farm town garage bands. My Brian Epstein just never showed up.

So I waited patiently. To avoid getting a full-time job that would cut too deeply into my music time, I went to college. After college, I found jobs mostly so people would stop asking me when I was going to get a job.

I told myself it would still happen. I checked the ages of everyone on the pop charts, finding the ones older than I. I switched from rock to country-folk, a style of music in which people past 30 could still get famous.

Everyone around me assumed I had accepted the inevitable, that I had settled down, that I had fallen back. But I knew better.

One night at an open mike night at an Irish bar in Washington, D.C., a college girl with the soul and voice of a poet had taken her turn at the mike, and so had I.

"I'm gonna give music one more year," she said, as we leaned against the bar. "And if I don't make it by then, I'm putting away my guitar."

Then she asked how long I was going to try before I gave up.

"I'm never giving up," I answered. "I think if I spend my whole life trying to get famous, and never do, that's better than anything else I could ever do with the rest of my life."

Of course, those were the days when it never occurred to me that I wouldn't be famous one day.

It wasn't until 10 years after that, when I got the job I have now, that I did exactly what I told the girl in the bar I would never do.

Over the past few years I have convinced myself that I was just never in the right place at the right time. Oh, cursed fate that shines on the few and rains on the rest of us!

But here's what I thought today on the Magical Mystery Tour bus: There couldn't have been a righter time or place than Liverpool in the early 1960s. Once the Beatles showed how easy it was to pry money from the pockets of teenagers, record companies ran toward the little dock town of Liverpool like lemmings to a C-note. Bands that had been paying their dues for years were signed. Brand new bands were signed. Gerry and the Pacemakers. The Searchers. The Foremost. The Merseybeats.

But if Liverpool was the right time and place, how do you account for the wall of fame? Gerry of Gerry and the Pacemakers dedicated it a few years ago. Each brick in the wall of a bar on the street where the Cavern used to be features the name of a band that used to play there.

And even I, who pride myself on knowing a ridiculous amount of "British Invasion" trivia, never heard of most of them.

Could it be that they just weren't as good as the Beatles?

Oops.

You may not have felt it, friends, but I just skated onto thin, cracking ice.

What if I never got famous because I was just never as good as I thought I was? Where does that leave me, now that I'm knocking on 50's door? How do I swallow such a ragged, bitter pill?

Tonight I am thinking that fame for me is like that person whom you loved more than she loved you. When I think of it, my heart hurts for a minute. Part of that hurt is because I wonder if I gave up on music too soon, or was never really that talented in the first place. I think I'll always wonder.

To lift myself out of that slough of despond, I run a quick mental tally sheet.

Here's what I don't have: fame, enormous wealth, busloads of people taking photos of the Western Auto where my father bought my first set of drums.

Here's what I have: a heart full of memories with a woman who loves me; a son I love more than life; a job that is creatively stimulating, pays well and, as a bonus, is a whole lot of fun; a music collection that includes every song the Beatles ever recorded; and a guitar I've owned since 1972.

Sometimes I take out that guitar and sing with a bunch of other people who always assumed they'd be famous. It's fun. Recently I wrote a song about my son, and when he heard it, he hugged me and told me he really liked it. That was really fun.

So guess what?

I win.

To celebrate my victory, I'm going to give myself an early birthday present. Tomorrow, when I rail south out of Liverpool, I'm leaving the dream here, where it belongs.

OK. Here are a few ways to pass the time if you ever happen to be into your second hour of sitting on the ground in a plane in London waiting to take off.

Listen to "Layla" by Derek and the Dominoes on the plane's headphones. Supposedly, Eric Clapton wrote this song for his then-girlfriend Patti, who was married to Clapton's good friend George Harrison. Which only proves again that everything on Earth is Beatles-related.

While listening to Derek and his friends, watch rerun after rerun of *Everybody Loves Raymond* on the plane's movie screen. Apparently Great Britain loves *Raymond* too. They probably think Ray is a bloody-right bloke. Watching without the sound will prove once and for all that Doris Roberts and Peter Boyle are every bit as entertaining with the sound off.

Or you could talk to perfect strangers about the toilets in England. They're very deep. The toilets, not the strangers. And a virtual Niagara is unleashed when you flush. You might also discuss the way neither of you heard anyone in England call a bathroom a "loo." Or a bathroom. Or a restroom. They always call it a toilet. Obviously, when you have something that impressively deep…

And, by the way, you know that pain you get in the base of your back about the second hour of a long plane flight? You can get that before you ever leave the ground!

So, as long as you're stuck here with me anyway, here's something that happened in the airport while I thought I was waiting the last few minutes before taking off for home. Oh, how I long for those innocent times again.

An American girl wanted to use British coins to buy a Kit Kat bar from a vending machine in the waiting room at Gate 20.

She had a two-pound coin, but those are big and cool and impressive looking—like the British toilets of coindom—and she wanted to save it to impress the kids back home.

All of us minding our own seats and hiding in our respective books could hear her and her mom counting out her other British coins. And we heard when her mom said, "You're nineteen pence short."

I had some cute English coins in my pocket that I was taking home for Aaron to take to show-and-tell, so I took out a twenty-pence coin and offered it to the mom.

Hey, I know the strength of a candy bar jones.

The young girl thanked me and went to the snack machine.

No Kit Kat.

"Did you use five-pence coins?" asked a friendly English voice from another row. "Because it won't take the five-pence coins. They go straight through."

Then began a remarkable effort by a number of strangers to make sure this American girl, whom none of them knew from Eve, got the right coins for her candy bar.

"I've got 50p."

"Here's a pound."

And when she got the candy bar, it was to the sound of a "Good job!" and an "All right!" and some scattered applause.

She sat next to her mom, beaming. Strangers smiled as a

couple of toddlers played nearby and a mother strolled by with a baby in a carriage.

And I thought, we are exactly the same as the people who got on those planes on September 11th.

And now Willie Nelson sings into my headphones, "If you fall, I will catch you…time after time."

And I feel an immense, overwhelming need to be home. Hour three begins.

TO THE PLACE WHERE i BELONG

Anyone who says you can never go home again has never driven to Pennsylvania with me.

BABY, I CAN DRIVE MY CAR

I spent 10 hours alone in a car today.

And yes, I was driving.

So it's been a long day, and if you don't mind, I'm gonna go George Carlin on you for a moment. Here are some scattered bits of advice, odd observations, and a question:

1. If you're even close to my age and you're going to drive for 10 hours, stop at every rest stop, even if you think you don't have to go. Trust me. You have to go. We always have to go. I have to go just talking about it this long.

Even if you don't have to go when you turn into the rest stop—and remind me to tell you sometime about the man who turned into a rest stop—you'll have to go by the time you park the car and walk inside.

If you're really, really sure you don't have to go, just go ahead and try to drive past the rest stop. The instant you are past the off ramp, your bladder will fill up faster than a college bar on ladies' night, and you'll spend the next hour in agony waiting for any place you can pull over. Plus, the road will be bumpy.

An added bonus: if you stop at every rest stop, you can look like an aged dork by reaching for the sky to stretch your back and prancing around like a pink flamingo to stretch your knees, all the while emitting loud, self-satisfied groans.

This drives chicks wild.

2. Swallow your pride, and buy the pillow for the driver's seat. Your butt will thank you. Not literally, of course. But wouldn't it be cool if it did?

3. If you're going to play God, get it right. I saw one of those billboards that have a saying that they attribute to God. This one said, "Don't make me come down there." The thing is, most of the Christians I know would be delighted if God would come down here. If they could make God come down here, they would. That's what they're waiting for.

In my head right now I hear Jerry Seinfeld, and he's saying, "How does God pay for those billboards? Does the billboard company take a personal check? Do they ask for two forms of ID? Why did I walk away from the TV show?"

OK, I'm back. Here's what I wonder when I see those billboards: Is God really a big fan of sarcasm?

4. If you ride in a car for a long time, something will hurt. You never know what it will be, and you might be surprised. Your eyebrows might hurt from squinting all day. The outside of your knee might hurt from leaning against the door. The pain might hit the joint in your thumb from steering. Maybe your bladder will ache because you drove past the entrance to a rest stop. For me on this trip, it's my right heel.

Sure, you're thinking, "That's his accelerator foot." But the thing is, I hardly used the accelerator. I'm a cruise control guy. Love the cruise control. I'm also one of the last surviving speed limit guys. Whatever the speed limit is, that's what the cruise is set on.

This doesn't work in Indiana. Those wacky Hoosiers set a 65-mile-per-hour speed limit for me and a 60-mile-per-hour speed limit for semi-trucks. So I keep finding myself way too close to the big-letter sign on the back of the truck that explains how I can become a driver and make big money. I am forced to take the car out of cruise-o-matic so I can either brake or speed up and pass. This rankles me because it's so difficult to find the sweet spot on cruise control. You're always either a mile above the speed limit, or a mile below.

So the blister on my right heel remains unexplained.

5. Two words: AM radio. Unless that's three words. There is buried treasure for the taking if you leave the books on tape at home with the CDs and just keep hitting the seek button on the AM dial. Real people live out there, and they live on AM radio.

Today I heard:

•A local station with the news motto "When news breaks out, we break in." All I could think of was a second-story man with acne.

•Randy Newman singing "I've Been Working on the Railroad."

•A radio drama titled "The Doctor Fights," in which Gregory Peck treats German prisoners during the Second World War with the new miracle drug, Penicillin, and convinces them that Hitler is full of hooey to boot.

•A three-song birthday tribute to Brian Setzer.

•Bingo being played on the radio, with an announcer who kept explaining that for legal reasons, they couldn't actually call it Bingo.

•The Red Sovine song "Daddy's Girl," in which a little girl sings that her daddy must love her because he loves her like a son.

•A commercial for allergy medicine using the Who's "We're Not Gonna Take It" as background music. Why buy allergy medicine if you're not gonna take it?

•Les Nessman reading the news while beating on his chest to sound like a helicopter.

OK. So I made one of those up.

6. About hour five, I realized that it must be a little earlier in the year than when I usually drive from Kansas City to Pennsylvania. Usually all I see is green. This time I'm seeing mostly brown. Brown is underrated. It's actually a nice, soothing color. Lots of cool things are brown. Chocolate. Mud pies. My brown corduroy pants.

7. On Route 64, between the Missouri border and Santa Claus, there's a house with several huge replicas of World War II airplanes on poles in the front yard. You should be sure to look at it. It's an interesting change from the brown.

Not that there's anything wrong with the brown.

Santa Claus is the name of a town in Indiana, by the way. The exit for Santa Claus is listed on the same sign as Jasper and Ferdinand. So I'm guessing they all must be in "All Towns Must Be Named After Guys" county.

Just a ways farther down the road, I passed Brush Heap Creek. Now there's a self-image problem waiting to happen.

"Where you from, bub?"

"Got a little place down on Brush Heap Creek."

"Oh. How…um…nice."

Too much accuracy can be a bad thing. I don't call my living room the "Pokémon Toys on the Floor" room.

8. Here's the question I mentioned when I started this: If you kill enough bugs with your car windshield, can you start referring to yourself as "The Exterminator"? Because that's a cool nickname.

WHERE MY THOUGHT'S ESCAPiN'

It was taking longer than I thought it would to get where I was going, and I was tired and stiff. That spacey feeling had set in, the one you get from trying to fool your body into thinking it's been sitting still all day and not hurtling through space at 70 miles per hour. I was hungry but didn't want to take time to stop and eat, so I was rumbling inside my stomach and grumbling inside my head.

It was then that the message of hope appeared.

There, painted on a bridge just ahead, were the magic words: "Welcome to Pennsylvania." I surprised myself by starting to smile and was even more surprised when that smile turned into a big goofy grin as my car passed under the bridge.

That was yesterday, on my way to Gettysburg. This morning I drove through that lovely old town, where every other building is a bed-and-breakfast or a T-shirt shop. I cruised past farms and open fields and headed north on Route 15. I turned on the AM and hit the seek button, and the first song out of the radio was "She Loves You."

The road was lined with stone fences and hedgerows, crumbling barns and old, whitewashed brick buildings with 18-something painted on them. Occasional yellow forsythia would blaze out of the brown trees, along the divided highway that I remember as a two-lane road, hugging the beautiful

Susquehanna River. Like me, the river was not quite completely shed of its morning fog.

As I drove again on an old familiar highway and sang along with the Beatles, I decided that the reason West Virginia is "almost heaven" is that you have to drive north into Pennsylvania to actually reach the "Promised Land."

Look, I know I go overboard about Pennsylvania. It's just dirt and trees and buildings and highways, like every other state. My feelings for it have less to do with the state itself than with the fact that I grew up there.

But I can't help myself. It's just such a lovable old curmudgeon of a state.

At most of the intersections in Gettysburg—and in most other Pennsylvania towns—you will see the same sign: "No Turn on Red." Let the rest of the states fall for this new-fangled "right on red" idea, Pennsylvania seems to say. In this state we stop at red lights, buster, and we stay stopped until they turn green. Always have. Always will.

After driving across half the country, Pennsylvania was the first state I came to with a long stretch of 55-mile-per-hour road. All the other states had posted speed limits of 60, 65, even 70. Doesn't matter. William Penn is holding tight to his double nickels.

Driving a full day at 65 or 70 makes 55 feel like being parked on the highway. But it was OK. I came to Pennsylvania to slow down.

In Pennsylvania, they take care of you whether you want them to or not. They post little signs along the highway telling you what to do. "Watch for aggressive drivers!" "Don't tailgate!" "Trucks, right lane only!" "Use seat belts next million miles!" That last one is real, by the way. Somebody on the sign squad has quite the little sense of humor.

I marvel at the honest, sloppy beauty of this state, where a restored 150-year-old brick building sits next to a field of junked cars, all framed by a deep background of dirt-road lined hills and sleeping forests.

It might surprise you, then, to know that I don't consider Pennsylvania home. I used to. It was home while I was growing up here, and for several years after. But not now.

It's one of the good parts about having a few years under your ever-lengthening belt. You get a little older, you live through some stuff, and one day you realize that you are no longer your parents' kid but have instead become a freestanding human being in your own right.

That's not the same as leaving home for the first time, for college or work or whatever. I think most of us put on a brave face when that happens, but inside we secretly long to run back to the rooms of our childhood to read comic books.

But when we do go home again, on holidays, we are surprised to find the bed a little too short, and we worry about coming in too late, and we know that what was once our house is now the home of our parents.

So begins the long period of rootless wandering, not a kid, not a grown-up, always trying to accomplish something, but not sure what it is. Finishing college doesn't get us there. Buying a house doesn't get us there. Neither do marriage or children of our own. There's something, it seems, that we're just not getting right. One puzzle piece that has slipped behind the couch cushion.

The final answer, I think, is the answer to so many of life's little problems: Time. One day you just stop scurrying.

I don't know when that day was for me. But in the past few years, I've been able to stop trying to get somewhere and just realize that where I am is pretty nice. I've stopped denying the many mistakes of my past and am trying instead to just accept them as part of the deal. I treasure all of my memories but, even more, I treasure the day.

The past is a cool place to visit, but I wouldn't want to live there.

So I visit Pennsylvania like an old friend now. When you see someone you went to high school with, and they've grown a head of gray hair, it's surprising. Well, my little hometown has grown a McDonald's, and that's every bit as surprising. It's fun to come back here and catch up, to remember, to wake up in Pennsylvania again.

But every time I have typed the word "home" in this little ramble, I have seen the same thing in my mind: my wife and son.

I love visiting my little town and seeing my family again.

And when I'm done, I'll go home.

THERE ARE PLACES i REMEMBER...

I gotta get me one a them time machines.

Here's why: Every now and then I come to Pennsylvania, and when I do, I visit the sites that hold important places in my memory. More and more in recent years, when I go to those buildings, they are gone. In their places are parking lots or video stores or fast-food joints. All fine things, of course. Just not what I remember.

So today I thought I'd just drive around to some of the places I remember fondly and take pictures of them before they're gone. I especially wanted to get pictures of some of the places the garage rock bands of my teen years used to play.

After all, I fully intend to bore my son with those stories when he gets a little older and hardier.

I wondered, as I nosed the Chrysler down the road, how many of the buildings from 30-some years ago would still be standing. Especially since I sometimes wonder how I'm still standing.

I stopped off first at Troy Skateland. At least I assume it's still Troy Skateland. The big sign across the top that used to say "Troy Skateland" is no longer there. The building's there, though, so I took a picture of it because I feel fairly certain that someday soon it will be gone.

It was there that my older sisters used to take me skating on

Friday nights, and I would wobble around and around the floor to the echoing noise of the Four Seasons singing "Dawn." That's how I spent a lot of weekends until a few years later when they started having sock hops there with live bands, and I stopped skating. It was so much cooler to just stand close to the band and lean on a post. Especially since my hair was already longer than any of the guys in the big, fancy out-of-town band.

Later I played there myself, in two bands: Duck Soup and Ugly Elizabeth. Both were about average, as small-town bands go, but it didn't really matter. The acoustics are so bad in a skating rink that all the sound mushes together like oatmeal with feedback anyway.

While I was taking the picture, I stared wistfully at the basketball net, remembering the time I scored there.

Not at basketball, of course. I'm only five foot eight and a half. But it was there I kissed the first girl I ever kissed, right under the basketball net, as we walked around holding sweaty hands outside the sock hop.

The month was May, the girl was June, and I was an august swain. I was almost 14. She was almost 13. It was almost heaven.

Next, across to Mansfield, on a road I probably hitchhiked a hundred times, back in the days when you could do that sort of thing.

I parked my car in town and walked up the steep hill—steeper than I remembered it—to a student gathering place at the very top. I think it's called The Hut.

It's the first place that ever hired me when I turned from rock and roll to folk singing. They hired me without an audition—which is why they hired me—and paid me 75 dollars. I had a black Epiphone guitar then and thought I was John Prine. I wasn't.

On my way down the hill, I checked to see if Maple B student dorm was still there, and it was. Maple B was the college home of the first girl to watch me break my own heart and then blame it on her, back in the dark ages of the early 1970s.

Left at the light and over the hill in Mansfield will take you to the lovely little town of Wellsboro. When I was 15, after I'd played in two or three bands based in my hometown of Troy, I lucked into an out-of-town band called the Modds. It was the first band I just sang in, without playing drums. This was cool because I could show off more if I wasn't behind a drum set, plus the Modds had a drummer who was better than I was, although I didn't tell him that.

My Troy friends and I used to drive to Wellsboro to dances upstairs at the American Legion Hall, on the mistaken assumption that we would be far more attractive to girls from another town. A couple of my bands—the Fourth Regiment and the Funny Company—had even played there. Once each.

I have great memories of playing at the Wellsboro Legion Hall with the 13th Hourglass, which is what the Modds became after I joined them.

I didn't expect the building to still be standing—it was an old building in 1968—and if it was still standing, I doubted I could find it.

Still, I walked to where I vaguely remembered it should have been. There was a modern-looking suite of buildings. I walked around to the front and broke into a huge grin. The exact same huge wooden door fronted the building. I poked my head inside, and there was the same huge inner door leading up the steps to the hall where we played.

It was open so I looked around its edge. The two flights of steps leading up the dance floor were exactly the same. I half expected to see an empty Fruit Stripe gum wrapper or half-full bottle of Tab.

No one was looking, so I trespassed in and snuck up the two flights of stairs. I peeked around the torn sheet of plastic that hung across where the entryway used to be.

Almost 35 years later, it looked remarkably the same. It was still a wooden-floor hall, still exactly the same shape. Even better, there was a stage at one end, and that stage had amplifiers on it, just waiting for guitar plugs.

It looked pretty much exactly as it had the night Dave the bass player and I kicked jack-o'-lanterns off the edge of the stage and changed the words to "Born To Be Wild" to "Get your pumpkin runnin'…head out on the pumpkin."

You wish you could have been there, don't you? I know. We all have our disappointments.

The thing about that dance hall that had changed is that now it's a Christian club for teens. Instead of bare, peeling walls, there are now peeling walls with Bible verses and pictures of Jesus on them.

I was delighted to see it. This is one circle that remains unbroken.

I walked up the road to the house where Bill the guitarist used to live and where the band hung out in those days. Now, it's a lovely little home, wearing a fresh coat of paint and a close-trimmed lawn. I'm sure that the family living there has no idea that the guys once played the classic "put his hand in warm water while he's sleeping" gag on me, or that the spot on the carpet was the result.

Then it was up the back roads through Keeneyville and Shortsville to Cowanesque, where we played at the high school once, I think. I went through Knoxville, and as I passed a brick building on my left, I said to myself, "Hey, that's the teen center where we used to play!"

And maybe it was. I also wouldn't be surprised to learn that the building I saw wasn't even built in the late '60s. I've learned to doubt some of my more uncertain memories.

No doubt about this next one though. Elkland, Pennsylvania, is the home of the Elkland Fire Hall, where I auditioned for the Modds in 1968 and failed the audition, even after my big finish—a breathy rendition of the Bee Gees' "To Love Somebody."

They called me back three months later for another shot at it.

I ended my day's sojourn in Corning, New York, where I learned that, alas, the Rat Hole is a parking lot now. The Rat Hole was a typical college apartment house, which meant it was a dump. Bill from the band and my great friend Truman lived there, so the band was there most of the time on weekends too.

Their apartment was furnished with a table and two chairs in the kitchen and mattresses on the floor in the other two rooms. There was a refrigerator, which may have been designed for something besides beer, but that's all it ever held. On the wall was a long running tally in pen for the game of Gin Rummy that was constantly going on.

And now cars park on that corner. No historical marker or anything.

The store in Corning where I bought the Ovation guitar I still play is gone now too.

Thank goodness Wet Goods is still there.

I started going to Wet Goods when I was way too young to be there. It's a bar, after all, and I started sneaking in at age 16, two years under the legal age. I drank dark beer, which actually tasted just as bad as regular beer but was a lot cooler to order because you could say, "Large dark, please."

A few years later, when I entered my troubadour stage, I went back to Wet Goods to play folk songs and pass the hat. I was one of a tight circle of half-a-dozen or so other Gordon Lightfoot-wannabees with acoustic guitars.

Wet Goods was owned by a man named Bob, who could have been Ernest Hemingway if the job hadn't already been taken. He looked like one of Santa's elves, with his silver hair and beard and that roguish twinkle in his eyes. He painted, sculpted, loved Vivaldi, and was the best friend a bunch of usually broke folk singers ever had.

Most of us wound up tending bar at Wet Goods for extra money at one time or another, and several of us lived off and on in second stories of buildings Bob owned. I don't know how old he was in the 1970s, when I sang there, but he was older than any of us.

And I found out during my visit to Wet Goods that he's still around, working at a winery further upstate.

A woman, smoking in an afternoon shaft of daylight at the end of the bar, brought me up to date with some of the others who sang and passed the hat at Wet Goods in the early 1970s. One is a lawyer, one is a teacher, and another is a minister. One was scheduled to play folk songs at Wet Goods the following weekend.

The only folk singer she didn't remember was me.

Ouch.

Wet Goods looked remarkably, satisfyingly similar to the last time I was there. I felt like I was spending time with an old friend.

All in all, a fine day. Still, it left me strangely empty.

The thing is, I don't really want to visit places from my past. I want to visit my past. I don't want to live in the past, but, gee, it would be cool to go back there for quick visits once in a while.

So, back to the time machine thing I mentioned earlier.

I would never want to see the future. I figure if it's bad, I'd just dread it, and if it's good, I'd just be dissatisfied with the present. But I wouldn't mind visiting the past.

Although…

If I went back to my past looking like I am now, I doubt that any of the people I'd want to see would want to have anything to do with me. Are they really going to let some mostly bald gray-haired old guy grab the mike and tear into "Brown Sugar"? Doubtful.

And if I went back in time and was the same age as I was then, wouldn't I be plagued by all the naiveté and insecurity I had to struggle with then?

Or if I went back and was the age I was then, but knew what I know now, well wouldn't that just make me kind of a spooky cat-dog character, who didn't really fit in on either side of the kennel?

Maybe it's better if I enjoy the good memories, accept the bad ones, and just ease on, ease on down the road.

2-GOOD 2-BE 4-GOTTEN

When I mentioned to one of my work friends that I was going to stop by my old high school to look at all of the yearbooks that have pictures of me in them, she said, "Taking along an X-ACTO knife?"

I'm not one of those people who get all wrinkly-nosed and red-faced when I see old pictures of myself. I know I was a weird-looking kid. I wallowed in being a weird-looking kid. Bring on the weird, I say.

So, for an hour today I sat in a wooden school chair in a little room off the library, which was the gym when I was a student there, and looked at the Troy High School yearbooks from 1964 through 1970.

The first thing that struck me was how wrong people's perceptions of the 1960s are. Even mine, and I was there.

Right through to 1970, most of the boys in the yearbook photos have short, side-parted hair, plaid shirts with button-down collars, and straight-leg jeans or slacks. Most of the girls have short perms and, although the Brenda Lee end-flips were a lot more prevalent in the earlier years, they were still around in 1970. So were those pointy-cornered glasses with rhinestones on them.

Often, people associate the '60s with hippies, and they associate hippies with brilliant flashes of neon color. The yearbooks are almost completely in black and white, and it seems appropriate, like a rerun of *Leave It To Beaver* or *Father Knows Best.*

It is 1967 before a flowered shirt shows up among the madras. A year later for paisley.

I didn't grow up in a town of love-ins, peace marches, and rock festivals, but one of football games, the annual town fair, and Friday night roller-skating.

For the 1960s, we stayed remarkably in the 1950s.

Even the friends of mine who loved rock and roll and the Beatles almost as much as I did were a pretty conservative bunch. The primary difference between them and everyone else in the yearbook is that their hair is combed an inch down their foreheads, rather than being sharply parted to the right or left.

In the 1965 yearbook is a picture of the Chess Club. Three of the members were kids who played in rock and roll bands I was in. A lead guitarist was a junior high class officer. A bass player also played football.

One of the reasons I had to visit my old high school to view yearbooks was that I never bought any of them.

For me, high school was enjoyable but unimportant. Troy was just the town I was going to leave, as soon as the suede cowboy boots I wore to graduation could carry me away. They didn't understand me there. They didn't respect me there. They couldn't see what was ahead for me the way I could see it.

Let the others take over their father's farms, or go to Mansfield or Penn State to college, or get married and start cranking out future Troy High School graduates. I had bigger plans.

My little town seemed content to pretend that there wasn't a larger world. I knew better. I wasn't reading *16* magazine for nothing.

I could see pictures of the cool fashions that the Ben Franklin in Troy didn't sell. I knew about Beatle cuts. I knew there were rock and roll managers out there just waiting to sign me, record companies just waiting to record me, fans just waiting to mob me.

Like so many kids in so many little towns, I resented Troy for holding me back.

So it's interesting, looking through those old yearbooks, to realize how much fun I had in school. A surprising number of my teachers were cool. I'd forgotten that until I saw their pictures again.

The photos of the senior play and the senior talent show reminded me of what a great time the rehearsals were. That brought to mind my junior high production of *Romeo and Juliet,* and I grinned like a smiley button. Other photos reminded me of my completely forgotten membership in the drama club.

I thought about the poem I wrote when my English teacher asked for an essay and how she read it to the whole class. I remembered the math teacher who taught one-to-one correspondence with such humor and enthusiasm that, to this day, I remember the phrase "one-to-one correspondence." I thought about elephant jokes and cinnamon fireballs, about doing the Twist and the Freddie in the gym, and about a pretty, blond girl in a plaid miniskirt, held shut with a huge gold pin, worn over textured stockings.

I thought of a thousand little conversations in front of lockers or in line at the chocolate milk machines. I remembered strutting down the broken, uneven sidewalks into town while my friend Jack sang self-penned dirty versions of Top 40 songs.

After my library research, I walked down the hallways of my old school. I was walking against a sea of students on the way to their next classes, and I thought about how lucky they all are.

The girls can wear pants to school, instead of the skirts or dresses girls were required to wear when I was in school. They can all wear shorts, which were, of course, completely unheard of, unless you were putting up prom decorations that day.

And, they're lucky because one of these days they'll have a fine collection of memories.

For somebody who couldn't wait to shake the dust of Troy, Pennsylvania, off my feet, I always enjoy coming back. Maybe we're not meant to know how good we have it during the actual having.

I know now.

ALL THE WORLD'S A HIGH SCHOOL AUDITORIUM STAGE

I found myself reminded of the great Dan Fogelberg line about "that old familiar pain."

Except his was a pain in the heart from seeing an old love again. My pain was in the middle left section of my back.

This particular ache is one that I hadn't felt in years. It can come from only one thing: Sitting in the wooden-back chairs of the Troy High School auditorium for more than five minutes.

I'm not sure who designed the chairs in my high school auditorium, but I'm pretty sure it wasn't anyone who was going to have to sit in them. I think if the people of Troy were to host some sort of a "thanks for designing our chairs" tribute, the designer would want it held someplace else. Someplace more comfortable.

During my high school years, I watched dance band concerts, heard lectures from the principal-of-the-moment, watched a visiting school drama club throw papier-mâché rocks at the conclusion of *The Lottery,* and sat through all two-plus hours of the movie *Shenandoah,* all in those torturous seats.

One thing I was pretty sure I wouldn't miss from high school was those chairs, and one thing I was pretty sure I wouldn't feel again was that old familiar pain in the back. Matter of fact, I had completely forgotten about it until a couple of nights ago, when my sister and I went to see the annual Troy Lions' Club Minstrel

Show. This year's hour of songs, dance, and jokes was "A Tribute to Rock and Roll."

I pride myself on knowing every old joke in the world and on being able to see the punch line coming on any new joke. It's my job to crack jokes, after all. I listen to jokes the way a plastic surgeon watches a beauty pageant: constantly comparing my work to somebody else's. So the six sidemen in this show, shouting jokes to each other from opposite sides of the stage, didn't surprise me very often.

They surprised me with this one, though:

A guy was eating in a fast-food restaurant when an elderly couple came in and ordered one cheeseburger, one order of fries, and a single drink. The guy thought they were too poor to get two meals, so he offered to buy them the other one. "No thanks," the lady answered, "We share everything." So he watched them and saw that while they took turns sipping the drink, only the man was eating the burger and the fries. So again he offered to buy them a second meal, and again the woman said, "No, thank you. We share everything." "Well," he answered, "I noticed that you're not eating. If you share everything, what are you waiting for?" And she answered, "The teeth."

About 45 people were on the small stage at one time or another during the show, which is an incredible number considering the size of Troy. Some of them, I imagine, just wanted to help the causes that small-town service groups like the Lions are involved in. Others were up there because they're in the club so they have to be. But I'll bet some of them were hams in search of a stage, any stage. This was their chance to be stars in their own hometown, and they broke legs for it.

I understand the lure of that little wooden platform in front of those rows of faces. I have a history on those boards myself.

I was the one in the white shirt and black dress pants that had creases as sharp as the pain in your back from sitting in those seats. The one beating on the bass drum in the junior high concert band the night we made the big time and got to perform in the high school. The one furiously chomping gum in time to the music and wondering why audience members were pointing to my face and giggling.

A few years later, I was the one sitting on the edge of the stage singing the Rolling Stones' "As Tears Go By," while my buddy Chris played guitar; and a few years after that, singing Dylan's "Positively 4th Street." That was my pal Mickey and I up there with another of my rock-and-roll friends, Pat, billed as "The Real Americans." Mickey was on guitar, Pat was on kazoo, and I played the spoons to "I'm a Yankee Doodle Dandy" and "Draft Dodger Rag."

Perhaps you saw Troy High's version of *Laugh-In* in 1969? That was me doing the Henry Gibson part. Here's my poem:

> Hang down your head, Tom Dooley.
>
> Hang down your head and cry.
>
> Hang down your head, Tom Dooley.
>
> Your necktie got caught in your fly.

And that was me sweet-talking Jenny, whom I actually had a little crush on. She was playing Granny, and I was playing Gaylord Merriweather Foxhall in our class production of *The Beverly Hillbillies,* directed by the affable and patient Mrs. B.

You must have heard about that one. It made the school newspaper.

So, anyway, I know the magic of that stage. I know what it is to walk out on rubber legs and try to impress a theater full of people who are fidgeting in an effort to keep their backs from hurting.

I am familiar with the exhilarating experience of having your friends compliment you the next day—maybe sincerely, maybe not—and even having complete strangers say "Saw you up on stage the other night."

One of the great things about a small town is that to the people in the audience, for that one brief moment, you really are a star, just because you're on that stage while they're in those seats.

I was glad I got to see it happen for 45 people from my little town. I was particularly pleased to see that a lot of them were my age or older. This gives me hope that I, too, might always be able to find a place to show off.

I know myself well enough by now to know that I will always prefer being onstage to being in the uncomfortable seats.

FOOLISH ON THE HILL

Every now and then I feel the need to do something physically foolish to prove to myself that I am not yet a retired mustard-cutter. While visiting my old haunts in Pennsylvania, I decided to hike the rim trail at Buttermilk Falls.

The rim trail goes straight up into the hills approximately forever before leveling off at the top. It's a fairly easy trail for kids, athletes, and dogs, but a little harder for me. I was walking at a pretty good clip for a guy my age and sweating at a pretty good clip as well.

So, at the top, I sat down and panted a while, staring down the hill to the river that led to Buttermilk Falls far below.

Even with no leaves on the trees, it was beautiful up there. It was made even more perfect by the record-breaking 85-degree day.

My frantic panting slowed to a nicely regulated wheeze, and I began to relax. Being in the woods always calms me down a little, unless it gets dark and I start thinking about *Deliverance*. Dark was a long way off, and I couldn't hear any banjos, so I wasn't worried.

It occurred to me that the hill I was staring down was a larger version of the personal hill of my childhood.

That one is near the house I grew up in, and I spent a lot of time climbing around on it. Sometimes I went up on that hill when I was bored or if I felt like things weren't going my way at home. Sometimes I went because, growing up with two brothers and two sisters, it was nice to just be alone for a while.

To get to my hill, I climbed out of the bedroom window and jumped off the porch roof, walked across the lawn, then through the field where we kept the pigs, then past the barn surrounded by long-retired automobiles full of mice and spiders. Finally I tromped through the pasture owned by the neighbor up the road and into the edge of the woods.

Off to my right a ways was the little round marsh, where the toads sang and the skitter-bugs danced. Off in the distance on my left were the birch trees, softwood that broke off at the base and fell against each other at angles so a kid could walk up them without using his hands.

There was a bald spot 15 minutes or so up that hill. When I reached it and sat down, I could see clear across the valley.

Today, sitting up there on the ridge above Buttermilk Falls, I closed my eyes for a minute and thought about what I would see if I were on the hill behind my house again.

In one direction would be the house of the neighbor who told me that when the wind was just right, he could hear me singing in my front yard half a mile away. I told him how sorry I was.

Across the valley in another direction would be the vacant lot where my uncle's barn used to be until it burned into the sky a couple of years after my cousin Buzzy died.

I thought about the strange ways of fate and circumstance. My cousin never got out of his teens, yet, 35 years later, I'm still around.

I had some wonderful daydreams while staring off that hill. I dreamed of catching the bad guys, of kissing my secret girlfriend, of having my chauffeur drive past the front of the house so I could show the other members of my world-famous rock band where it all began.

They were the kind of dreams that made bad days better.

When I went to my hill in those days, I thought about the future. Now, on a different hill, 50 miles and 35 years away, I think about the past.

There's just something about a wooded hillside that gets me thinking.

I don't climb my personal hill anymore when I visit Pennsylvania. None of my family lives in the house where I grew up, for one thing. For another, I've grown wary of walking across the connecting field and onto the hill, both owned by people who aren't me. Now that I own things, I've learned to respect the property rights of other people. I wouldn't want some old gray geehaw traipsing across my field just because he used to have a favorite hill on the other side.

Plus, I worry more than I used to about getting my shoes muddy.

But the hill by the rim trail at Buttermilk Falls made a nice substitute. I sat for several minutes, staring and thinking. Then I started to think about promises to keep and miles to go and sleeping.

That reminded me that it wasn't a snowy evening, but a beautiful, warm spring day. And, since I am so not Robert Frost, I sat and stared and thought a while longer.

ON THE BATTLEFiELD

While standing on a hill in Gettysburg, Pennsylvania, surrounded by the ghosts of Civil War soldiers, I started to cry.

I've noticed that I cry more often than I used to. I tear up over things that never used to get to me.

Maybe the brain cells that once held my feelings in check have all died from overuse. Maybe I'm just more emotional than I used to be. Maybe I'm just getting too old to care if I get caught crying.

So I was unable to stop my eyes from misting over when I read the words of the Gettysburg Address, which were written on a memorial about 300 yards from where Lincoln spoke them in 1863.

I didn't actually see any of the ghost soldiers that surrounded me, of course, even though they are rumored to sometimes visit my hotel just down the hill. But I could feel them everywhere.

That's not what choked me up.

It wasn't even the simple eloquence of Lincoln's few words or imagining what it must have been like to hear him say them on that hill.

I think I cried because of the sudden, painful realization that 140 years later, we're still a nation stained and weakened by the same kinds of prejudice that led to the Civil War.

The thing is, we were supposed to be past this. We were all supposed to be equal by now. And I can't help thinking it's my generation that was supposed to accomplish it.

When the boomers were teenagers, we claimed to believe all sorts of silly things. We said wars would end if people just didn't show up to fight. We said world leaders could get along if they would just talk to each other. We said that if we could just share the food, everyone on Earth would have enough to eat.

We said those things, but in our hearts, most of us probably doubted them.

But equality was something we were sincere about. We honestly believed that once we had the reins, prejudice would be gone.

It was, after all, so simple. All we had to do was be cool with each other. We could do that.

And as for racism, sexism, anti-Semitism, and all the other "isms" in the ism-book…they had no place in a utopia built on love, self-expression, and peaceful coexistence. Prejudice was the demon that haunted our fathers and mothers and grandfathers and grandmothers. Like so much of what the generations before us had believed, we weren't interested.

We knew prejudice was wrong. But even beyond that, we knew it was just really, really stupid.

So we planned to convince the friends our age who still told racial jokes or used anti-Semitic slurs that those things were no longer cool, and we knew they would listen to us, because we were right. We would make friends with people who were a different color than we were, or a different religion than we were, or a different nationality than we were; and everyone would see us making friends with them.

Heck, maybe even the old people from the generation before ours would see the errors of their ways. And if they didn't, well, we could just move into a better future without them.

Today, on a hill in Gettysburg, I wondered what happened.

An even better question: What didn't happen?

After all these years, why do we still talk a good game of equality while sitting on the sidelines watching intolerance?

And worse, when did people my age—the true believers—get in the "ism" game ourselves?

When did we start to think we could read people's thoughts and predict their actions based on the church they go to, or the part of the city they live in, or the language they speak, or whom they flirt with, or what they wear on their heads?

When did we decide to pass laws based on our own religious beliefs, and to hell with those who didn't share our views?

When did we decide it's OK to return anger for anger or greed for greed or hatred for hatred? Can we really justify those things just because we had to compete for jobs and scholarships?

Are we that selfish? Are we that small?

Was ending racism just another crazy idea from the goofy '60s?

I thought of these things, standing in Abraham Lincoln's shadow, and I cried.

This is us, people! This is our turn! We weren't supposed to perpetuate this garbage. We were supposed to fix this. We were supposed to change the world. The fact that we failed breaks my heart.

In Gettysburg, Lincoln said, "It is for us, the living, rather to be dedicated here to the unfinished work which they who fought here have so nobly advanced."

He also said, "The world will little note nor long remember

what we say here."

I fear another generation has proved him right. And this time it's mine.

*   *   *   *   *

A POSTSCRIPT: The morning after I wrote this, I got up and went jogging through the battlefields of Gettysburg. There are better ways to start a morning, but not many.

A lady who looked to be in her late 70s or early 80s was coming toward me, walking a happy, fluffy white dog along the road that runs past monuments to fallen Civil War soldiers.

"Well, hello!" she said through a huge smile. "Haven't seen you out here in a while! I missed you!"

I was jogging, so I was, of course, gasping for air.

"Sorry," I answered, trying to smile as wide as she was smiling. "You must mean someone else. I'm not from around here."

"Oh. Where you from, Honey?"

"Kansas."

"What part?"

I was tempted to do the old "all of me" joke, but decided not to put her through that. She was being nice, after all.

"A suburb of Kansas City, Missouri."

I thought it was impolite to keep jogging in place while we talked, so I stopped.

"Oh no," she said. "You just keep a-goin'. Have a nice day, now."

She was a black woman, walking her dog across a field where so many had fought for the right to buy and sell her ancestors, in a country where her dog would have had more freedom.

OK, so maybe as a society we've moved about a foot off the starting line. That's a good direction. We should keep a-goin'.

WHiZ ON DOWN THE ROAD

A rest-stop diary.

THURSDAY

1:16 p.m. The trouble with driving somewhere is you have to drive back, which I started to do one hour ago. Forget what I said about time machines. What I really want is an instantaneous matter transporter. Because, I gotta tell you, compared to a day and a half of driving to get home, going through life with the wing and head of a fly doesn't sound that bad.

2:02 p.m. Pretty close to Penn State now. I have two memories of Penn State. That's where I saw my first John Prine concert, and just down the street in State College is where I almost choked to death on a roast beef sandwich at a fast-food joint.

3:01 p.m. If you get so bored that you start naming roadkill along the highway in Pennsylvania, and if you're any kind of a Beatles fan at all, it won't take you long to use "Rocky Raccoon." Even if you're not sure what you just passed used to be a raccoon.

4:00 p.m. As a professional humor writer, it bothers me that I don't have time to scribble "wipe hands on pants" after the instructions on the hand dryers at these rest stops. I guess some other wacky prankster is just going to have to pick up the slack.

4:36 p.m. Just left Pennsylvania. So now I'll have to mentally prepare myself to whiz in Ohio for a while.

6:26 p.m. OK, apparently there are very long stretches of Ohio road with no rest stops. This is a cruel trick to play on a guy my age trying to crank out a lot of miles.

6:52 p.m. I've reached that dangerous point where I think I'll get from central Ohio to Kansas City a lot sooner if I just walk real fast from the car to the restroom and back. It's just a matter of time before I stop washing my hands. And you really don't want to know what comes after that.

7:46 p.m. I pulled into this rest stop just as "I Should Have Known Better" was ending, and I turned off the radio just as "Seasons in the Sun" was starting. So my timing is still good.

8:50 p.m. Every time I start this trip home from Pennsylvania, I always think I'll just drive all night and go straight through. Then it gets to be 8:50 p.m., and I know how nuts I was to ever think that.

10:15 p.m. Well, that was spooky and stupid. I mean, sure, it's possible that the couple I saw hanging out by the vending machines weren't undead vampires, but just barely possible. I don't think I'll be going into another highway rest stop after dark without one of Scully's flashlights. And Scully to carry it.

11:00 p.m. About the time I saw the jackalope run across the road in front of my headlights, I decided it might be time to find a motel.

FRIDAY

5:10 a.m. Indiana doesn't want me after all, so I'm back on the road again, with two songs stuck in my head.

7:44 a.m. I'm in a fast-food restaurant parking lot. The first Indiana rest stop I went past was closed. Thirty seconds past the "closed" sign was a sign that read "Prison area. Do not pick up hitchhikers." Coincidence? There was no other Indiana rest stop, and I had every intention to pull into the first Illinois rest stop and write something really nasty about Indiana. But the first Illinois rest stop was closed. The next one is 70 miles away. So I'm in a fast-food restaurant parking lot.

8:41 a.m. Do human beings have haunches? Because if they do, mine are getting really sore.

9:41 a.m. Hate the car. Hate the road. Hate the radio. Hate this rest stop. Hate it all.

10:15 a.m. Missouri. Right state, wrong side.

11:50 a.m. Gee, I thought I'd be a lot more tired by now. Unless I'm too tired to know how tired I am. Once I actually did drive this straight through. 23 hours. I have no memory of the final five of those hours, and when I got home, I was wearing a state trooper's hat, and my socks were on my hands. That's a joke. At least I think it's a joke. Maybe I'm more tired than I thought.

1:20 p.m. Can't write. Must drive.

3:17 p.m. The car is parked in my driveway. Course, I still have to walk all the way to the front door. Wish me luck.

PROTEST, POLITICS, AND PATRIOTISM: A VISIT TO WASHINGTON, D.C.

We were all so certain of the things we protested, so sure we had the answers—the right answers. But doesn't time have a way of continually changing the questions? What better place to reconsider than Washington, D.C.?

i CAN SEE RiGHT DOWN YOUR CHiMNEY

It doesn't take much to make me smile sometimes. This morning it only took five words.

"You have a window seat."

I've been flying some lately, but it seems like I haven't gotten to sit next to the window in quite a while. I sat next to a window the first time I ever flew, and it's always been a big part of the experience for me.

We rolled toward our appointed runway for so long, I began to wonder if I hadn't boarded a big car with wings by mistake. Then we turned, the G-forces kicked in, and we lifted off. The police car that had been right beside us all the way on an adjoining runway stopped, and began to fade into the distance.

And I watched it go because, did I mention, I had a window seat?

People below looked like ants, except without crumbs of bread in their mouths that were bigger than their heads. Cars looked like toy ant cars, and we flew over a field full of cows that looked like ants you could milk.

The plane leveled, and so did I, floating comfortably high above a pacified world. It was God's sketchbook, perfect, pristine. At least I could believe that for a moment, drifting so high above it all.

There are wars down there, and terrorists, and bad drivers on the freeways, and rude salesclerks, but I couldn't see any of that from my seat in the clouds.

Still, I know that down there, not up here, is where the action is, and where the joy is.

It's fascinating to me that each little game board house we flew over is full of people living actual lives.

It's almost prom time, and Chad still hasn't asked Tiffany to go. Bob's mortgage is due. There hasn't been enough rain for the crops. There's been too much rain for the crops. Peggy is pregnant again, and doesn't want to be. Meredith wants to be pregnant, and isn't. Tom got laid off. *Gilligan's Island* is on TV Land.

Through this green and brown jumble of land runs a long, slow river, taking a thousand years to smooth the ragged edges off rocks, the way flying this high smoothes the jagged edges off humanity.

A jet streaks by far below, going to where we just left. It looks to be moving a whole lot faster than we are. Did we get one of those dawdling pilots? Is he up there thinking about the people in the little houses far below when he should be flying the plane?

The houses are farther apart down there now, and one is way out by itself, like an outpost on the moon, like the farmhouse where Eustace and Muriel and Courage live.

And I wonder what will save the 11-year-old boy in that house, the way the Beatles saved me. Baseball? Piano? Fishing? Farming?

We're over a cloud bank and, as always, I start looking for faces in the formations. The only face I can make out in these clouds appears to be a howling demon from Hades. That's bad. Right, Doc?

Soon it's all clouds below us. It looks like a distant landscape where Will and Penny Robinson might run from space monsters. I keep looking for faces. I can't let the demon boy be the only one I see on the trip. Bad joss. Finally I spot the Grinch and a warthog.

The sun is shining up through the clouds, and they are almost too white to look at, like me dancing.

Two or three guys just got out of their seats to line up for the plane's bathroom, so I assume we'll be landing soon. It made me wonder if those stories you hear about lumps of frozen sewage from airplanes are true. Is there one down there now, ripping through those clouds, tearing through the roof of one of those little farmhouses, making the front page of the local four-page newspaper?

We are starting our descent now, back to the world where some of us started our descent long ago.

I look for old, familiar sites. There's the dome of the Jefferson Memorial. I see Arlington, and catch my breath at the rows and rows of graves. Then I see the Pentagon, and as I remember the horrible sight of it on TV, scarred and smoking, I stop breathing completely for a second.

The plane thuds down at Reagan National Airport.

I'm back.

LOVE/HATE AMERICAN STYLE

Since I lived in Washington, D.C., for three years in the 1970s, I figured I still knew perfectly well how to use the Metrorail system, thank you very much, so I didn't ask for help. Naturally, I messed up and found myself on the wrong train going the wrong way. I backtracked once, and then everything went fine.

The long escalator carried me slowly up, up toward daybreak, and when I could see out, I felt like I was meeting an old friend at what used to be our special place.

It was all there. The Smithsonian Museum buildings, the art galleries, the merry-go-round, the three-for-ten-dollars T-shirt vendors, the Capitol on the hill at the far end. I didn't even have to look over my shoulder to know the Washington Monument was back there, just like always.

Tourists like me were walking, gawking, and pointing; and because it was a Saturday, there weren't a bunch of political aides and lawyers in suits walking hurriedly through, annoyed at the tourists for being in the way.

Even though school isn't out yet, lots of the tourists were families with children.

One of the things I always loved about living in Washington was that it was constantly full of tourists. They made the town gentler and friendlier. They gave natives continuous opportunities to appear wise and helpful.

The tourists, of course, can't begin to outnumber the pigeons and squirrels, who actually own Washington, D.C. They just continue to let the rest of us hang around there because we drop food.

So in some ways it looked the same as when I lived there, or at least as when I last visited about 10 years ago.

It didn't feel the same, though. I suspect one of us has changed.

To be sure, things were happening as I walked around that reminded me of old times. The single, plaintive wail of a saxophone was sounding across the park, and I figured there was a street musician out hustling for change. That made me smile, even before I realized he was playing "Hey, Jude."

Ten minutes later I saw my first jogger running around the mall. That brought back memories. Most lunch hours there are almost as many joggers on the mall as pigeons. The joggers are neater, but the pigeons are a tad less self-righteous.

Finally, after about half an hour, I saw the site that made me realize I was really back. A dad on vacation was losing his temper with his kid.

"Stop crying! I told you we'll see the dinosaurs after we see the lunar lander!"

I don't fault him. I have used that voice myself when the joys of a vacation become a little too joyful.

I was still walking and was almost to the Capitol building when I realized what was making me uncomfortable. The mall looked, well, shabby. There were big spaces where no grass was growing, and there were dandelions and crabgrass and clover. In short, America's front lawn looked a lot like mine.

I could be looking in a rose-colored rearview mirror here, but I remember the mall area in our nation's capitol as being immaculate, trimmed like a kid's first big-boy haircut.

Now it just looks like another county fair.

I think that's a shame.

America and I have had a love-hate relationship over the past 50 years. Sometimes we got along, sometimes we didn't speak. Often I was rude, and sometimes it was justified. There were times we nearly hated each other.

In the past few years we've started talking again. Matter of fact, I've come to think the old gal's really something pretty special.

And I want the millions of tourists who visit Washington, D.C., to see that, to know how beautiful a place this is. Like all smitten men, I want my date to be the prettiest girl at the party. The ironic thing is that lots of the buildings in that part of D.C. are getting balcony-lifts and foyer-tucks. Because of that, they are covered in big, gray tarps, and supported by rusty scaffolding. One of these days it will all look great. But not today.

I continued walking up Capitol Hill, past the Capitol itself, and past the Senate office building where I spent one of the most unpleasant days of my life, going from office to office applying for work right after I got out of college.

In that part of my walk I saw the first lingering signs of terrorism. Many of the streets I routinely drove, walked, or bicycled down in the old days are now closed to traffic, blocked by huge slabs of concrete with police cars parked behind them.

I am compelled these days to see if places I used to hang out are still around, so I walked to where the Irish Pub "Gallagher's on the Hill" used to be. I went there to sing folk songs at an open mike night once a week for a couple of years.

It's gone, and my memory of exactly where it was is too cloudy to know what has taken its place.

I hopped the Metro again, and rode to Dupont Circle. When the metro line was built, the escalator that takes you up out of the stop was the longest in the world. We were all a little more impressive in those days.

You come up from the mines into a trendy, artsy section of D.C. that's full of shops and galleries and banks. Ubiquitous traffic circles surround little parks, each one home to a statue of a soldier.

You can walk from Dupont Circle to the White House, and I did, past the coffee shops and parking garages and downtown hotels.

Pennsylvania Avenue in front of the White House is one of the streets you can't drive down anymore. It's blocked on both ends and is now a pedestrian thoroughfare. It's a big improvement.

The tourists can take pictures of each other 'til the elephants and donkeys come home and never fear absentmindedly backing into traffic. The protesters are free to stage demonstrations in Lafayette Park and know that passing tour buses will not impede their messages.

I noticed on a billboard, for example, that earlier in the day that I was there, they had staged "The Million Marijuana March" in Lafayette Park to speak out for decriminalization. Wanna bet the phrase "Dude!" came up more than once?

Pennsylvania Avenue is a people street now. Good.

As I crossed in front of the White House, a small orchestra of violins, horns, and percussion had set up in the middle of what used to be a busy street and was aiming classical music toward the White House.

I saw a homeless man picking through a garbage can right in front the White House, and I thought about two kinds of people: The ones who would think it was bad that a homeless person was in front of the White House, and the ones who would think it was bad that a person in front of the White House was homeless.

And speaking of the White House, I couldn't help notice that, while guards stop people from getting too close, pigeons and squirrels have no trouble going right through the gates and right up to the president's window.

Not that I'm suggesting that pigeons and squirrels are spies. Still, I wouldn't put it past them.

I was awestruck by the White House. Just knowing that behind that gate, behind those walls, President Jed Bartlett was sitting somewhere in the West Wing...

Well, I can dream.

The most inspiring thing I saw on my three-hour walk around Washington was something I noticed as I crossed the Mall again, heading toward the Metro stop. A light rain was falling in the insistent dusk, and I was looking at the Washington Monument. Behind it, a jet was descending toward the airport. As I watched, the jet disappeared behind the monument, reappeared on the other side, and kept going. I recalled a time not long ago when jets weren't allowed to fly there.

It was a stunning testament to this nation's orneriness and strength. The Mall in Washington, D.C., seemed exactly the right place for it. And it was a stirring feeling to know that, after having been so savagely brutalized, we have struggled back to a kind of normalcy.

HOW i NEVER LEARNED TO STOP WORRYiNG AND LOVE THE BOMB

As I think of September 11th and our return to a "kind of nor-malcy," I realize how "normal" now carries with it the ever-present awareness and fear of the enemy. It reminds me of earlier times and other enemies.

I first started thinking about this when I was spending a lunch hour with *Goodbye, Darkness: A Memoir of the Pacific War* by William Manchester.

I like Manchester because he's a great writer and because I usually agree with his take on history. His book *The Glory and the Dream* is on my rereading shelf, a place of honor reserved for books I read again every couple of years.

I've been disagreeing more with his thoughts on the Pacific War. I assume he's correct and I'm not, since he was a Marine there at the same age I was singing protest songs in bars.

Today I was struck by something he wrote. So much so that my soupspoon froze in mid-flight.

He was writing about the way the Japanese soldiers hid in caves at the end of the war and would not surrender, and about the American soldiers killed in horrific ways trying to root them out. He writes:

> You think of the lives which would have been
> lost in an invasion of Japan's home islands—
> a staggering number of American lives but

millions more of Japanese—and you thank
God for the atomic bomb.

You thank God for the atomic bomb.

I've lived my whole life with the atomic bomb and its bigger, meaner neutron cousins. I've feared the bomb, ignored it, cursed it, made jokes of it, and written protest songs about it. I've never once considered thanking the Lord for it.

I was talking with a stranger on an airplane recently about turning 50. When the topic came up, the first words out of her mouth were, "I never thought I'd see 50. I thought I'd die in a nuclear war."

I knew exactly what she meant. It's a common, deeply held memory of those my age.

There are a lot of people my age or a few years older who clearly remember atomic drills and "duck and cover" exercises from when they were kids. I don't. It could be that we thought we were immune at Springfield Elementary. Why would the Reds waste perfectly good bombs on cows?

Or it could be that we, too, crawled under our sturdy, bombproof wooden desks at our teachers' behest, and I have forgotten all about it, the way I've forgotten all four years of high school Spanish.

Maybe I don't remember because it scared me, or maybe I don't remember because it bored me.

What I remember clearly is the subtle, underlying sense of doom that rode shotgun with my generation. I don't know of any people my age who didn't hold in some back closet of their hearts the fear of death by nuclear annihilation.

We bought our Beatles records; watched *Secret Agent;* went to parties; tried to get to third base, on and off the ball diamond; and did all the things young people are supposed to do. But there wasn't a minute that we didn't just assume we would eventually fall victim to the mushroom cloud.

It wasn't long into the '60s before the truth about nukes came out. There would be no "duck and cover." I don't remember exactly when I first saw the black and white footage of nuclear tests. But I clearly remember the terrible whirlwind that flattened trees and buildings, like nailing a sandcastle with a howitzer.

We began to learn that each of the hundreds of bombs pointed at us had far more bang for the billions than the bombs that ended World War II.

Clearly, crouching by the curb with our jackets pulled over our heads wasn't going to help.

I started listening more closely to the emergency broadcasting system tests on the car radio. I sat, my spine rigid, my arms tensed, pulling myself toward the edge of the seat with the steering wheel. I would exhale, finally, after that long minute of tone and the concluding announcement, "This has been a test…"

I have always had faith in human nature. It was only recently that I started to think there might be such a thing as pure evil, and I'm still not sure.

So I didn't think anyone was going to maliciously push the red button.

But I have also always had supreme faith in governments to screw up. I suppose that's a result of forming a lot of my opinions during the '60s, and having them proved correct by the Pentagon Papers and Watergate in the early '70s. Whatever the reason, there it was. I believed someone would make a mistake, and then that mistake would paint someone else into a corner, and everybody's future would suddenly be measured in minutes.

I remember being astounded when some people started saying the best way to end the Vietnam War was to "drop an apple on 'em." Were there really people in America so naïve as to think that would be the end of it? That we could use a nuclear weapon and not receive one from the Soviets in return?

There is one odd day that stands out in my nuclear memory. I was a student at Corning Community College in New York, going about my usual routine of ignoring professors and trying not to get caught staring at female classmates. I don't remember exactly how it started, but all at once the campus was buzzing with an insistent rumor: The bombs were on the way. There had been a misunderstanding, the rumor reported, and it had resulted in nuclear weapons being fired by both sides.

In that way people have of bracing rumors with concrete facts, it was said that the nukes would land at an exact time, about 20 minutes away. Washington would implode first, of course, then New York City. We would be consumed by the backwash.

It was too silly to be true, of course. Everyone in my little group of friends, sitting on the stone steps in front of the commons, knew that. The odds of the rumor being true were one in a million.

We made jokes about cutting the next class, of not having to do term papers or go to our evening jobs.

But somewhere in the joking, I found myself wondering what I would do if the world only had 20 minutes to live. That's what growing up in a world full of Armageddon weapons will do to a guy in his early 20s.

It's interesting to me that we have become less concerned with the prospects of nuclear war over the years, while the bombs themselves have become more dangerous. The collapse of the Soviet Union may have lessened the likelihood of all-out nuclear war, but it also increased the odds of splinter nations mishandling aging missiles, or just getting cocky with them.

Little countries that aren't us have nukes now. If they decide to use bombs against each other, how can it not escalate?

How long will it be before a terrorist buys a nuclear bomb from a salesman who's sure he's found a place to survive the results?

Clearly, it could still happen.

In "Masters of War," Bob Dylan sings about how the makers of bombs have threatened his children, "unborn and unnamed."

My son is both born and named, and deserves to one day mark his own 50th birthday in some absurd way.

So I pray our luck will continue and the bombs will hold their tongues until a wiser generation than ours silences them forever.

GROWN TO GRAVEYARDS, EVERY ONE

Books about the Second World War all tend to end the same way. We win and they lose.

Each book arrives at the preordained ending by following a path past the same markers: Hitler's rise to power, the invasion of Poland, the Battle of Britain, Pearl Harbor, Hiroshima.

I know this because for the past 10 years or so, pretty much every book I've read has been about World War II. Some tell the whole story, some are about specific campaigns or places or battles, some about the people who led our side or theirs.

I hope to read many more.

There are too many interesting stories in this conflagration that happened everywhere on Earth for almost 10 years and, in the end, changed everything forever.

I have a feeling you could single out any person who was alive in those years, tell that person's story, and I would find it interesting.

I read war stories because they make me feel fortunate.

In London I picked up a book about the Battle of Britain, written from the British perspective. It was full of people living dull, everyday lives, like mine, right up to the moment bombs started to fall on their houses.

It includes a story of a little girl who wakes up to find her house is a pile of rubble and that her mother, who was sleeping beside her, will never wake up.

Stories like that make me feel blessed when I pass my son's room and see him sleeping peacefully.

When I scrape ice from my windshield in a howling winter wind, I think of all the soldiers who lived outside in foxholes in exactly the same kind of cold.

When I look out an airplane window to the ground so far below, I think of scared 18-year-olds in B-17s.

The first book I read about World War II changed my thinking about war. I started the book thinking all wars were terrible and unnecessary. I finished the book thinking all wars are terrible, but some are necessary.

I am not a hawk. But because of those books, I am no longer a pacifist.

This boomer generation I'm part of has been spoiled a little along our journey. Our parents and other people of their generation had seen The Depression and war, and they were determined their children would live better lives.

We deserved better lives, they figured, because they had paid so much already.

As a result, many of us were coddled and kept from harsh reality through the 1950s, and many of us ran wild through the 1960s. We lived at home too long after college and chose to make no commitments to anything through our 20s. We were filled with righteous indignation when we were unable to fulfill our goals without working for them.

I believe we were able to indulge ourselves that way because tens of thousands of men died horrible, lonely deaths halfway around the world, just a generation before ours.

My grandfather served on battleships in the Pacific in World War II, as did his sons. My father was on a troopship on the way to Europe when the war ended. If Truman hadn't dropped the terrible atomic bombs, my father might have been one of the men called on to invade Japan. Which is to say he might never have become my father.

So I came here, to the Tomb of the Unknowns at Arlington National Cemetery, to pay my respects.

To reach this shady bench on this quiet hill, I walked a path past row after row of headstones. Many are small, modest, gray stone markers.

There is no apparent order to the graves. Vietnam is next to World War II, next to Korea, next to World War I. Kentucky lies next to Ohio, next to Italy, beside California. Wives and children are buried here. One headstone had one word—"Infant."

It is as jumbled and disorganized as warfare itself, as random as death.

There are too many stones here because there have been too many wars, necessary though some were.

It's a huge field of honor, but not infinite. I wonder how long it will be until there is no more room for fallen warriors at Arlington. And I think about how great it would have been if World War II actually had been the war to end all wars. Her surviving veterans could finish their hopefully long lives, then rest here, knowing sons or grandsons or daughters or granddaughters would never join them.

The hallowed grounds of Arlington would never again be torn open to receive war dead.

I am a child of the '60s. In my naïve, idealistic youth, I believed my generation would be the one to end wars. I underestimated the staying power of that determined horseman of the apocalypse.

All of us who flashed the two-finger peace sign and sang

"Give Peace a Chance" have had to come to terms with the truth.

The world remains a fragile place, where fools start wars and heroes must finish them.

WHAT BULLETS COST

Several years ago I wrote about my memories of the day President Kennedy died. I wrote about being on the playground in sixth grade at Springfield Elementary School when word started to spread among the kids. I wrote about how some of the boys speculated about what kind of rifle was used because they knew about rifles from deer hunting with their dads. I wrote about them looking through imaginary scopes, shooting at imaginary presidents. And I wrote about how my teacher's eyes misted over when he told us the news.

I've been quoting that story ever since.

I've tried to be straight with you folks, so I must tell you that I don't know if it happened that way or not. Maybe I heard about it on the bus or at home. Maybe they made some kind of announcement at school. I may have believed a few years ago that it happened like I said, but probably I just pretended to remember it that way because it made a good story.

It's become a cliché over the years that all who were alive the day John Kennedy got shot remember what they were doing when they heard the news. I don't. Not exactly.

I stopped by John and Bobby Kennedy's gravesites at Arlington, anyway, and said a little prayer for them because I believe they saved my life.

If the books and plays and docudramas about the Cuban

Missile Crisis are true, I think it was the Kennedy brothers who stopped a nuclear war.

I was 10 years old in October of '62, and I'm glad the world didn't get blown up. A lot of interesting things have happened in the 40 years since.

Around the grassy corner from JFK's gravesite is the final resting-place of his little brother Bobby. I was sad at John Kennedy's grave, but I didn't cry until I stood in front of Bobby's marker.

It reminded me of all the heroes my generation has lost to bullets.

I was too young to vote when Bobby ran for president, and too busy with important things to follow politics. But I liked Bobby.

He seemed cool. He was enthusiastic and energetic and alive, unlike the gaggle of grandpas who usually ran for president. He talked like us, and we felt that if not for the need to play the political game by the suit and tie rules, he would dress like us too. I figured he was the only presidential candidate who knew the Beatles' first names.

Mostly, he acknowledged us. It seemed like Bobby didn't see young people as kids to be herded to the card table in the living room so the grown-ups could talk business.

I felt especially bad standing by Bobby's grave because he never got a chance to be president. John Kennedy's death was horrible, but he died doing the one thing he had always intended to do. Bobby never got to.

I favor the underdog, so I always liked Martin Luther King Jr. He had taken on an impossible task, I figured, and he went at it steadfastly, with good humor.

They started making jokes about King early on in my little

world. Usually the jokes prominently featured the terrible word. Clearly, people were nervous about a black man who wanted to claim freedom and equality. The only way to combat it was to relegate him to the mass, to define him by the stereotype, to remove his individuality and, therefore, his humanity.

I grew up in a society where my father told me never to bring a black friend to our house. My mother, the liberal wing of the family, said there was nothing wrong with having black friends, but I should never date a black girl.

They were both products of their time, as were all of the people who surrounded me in childhood.

So I admired King quietly, privately.

As much as his stand on the equality of peoples, I admired the courage it took for him to resist responding to violence with violence.

In the end, when he refused to sit quietly in the back of society, when he refused to accept his place, the people who feared change so much killed him.

The people I knew who had been making all the jokes didn't celebrate or approve. They just shook their heads and said it was too bad but that he brought it on himself and should have known better.

Bobby and Martin's deaths were proof to my generation that the great and powerful "they" weren't going to let us in. Indeed, they were going to do whatever it took to keep us out. The system couldn't be changed by sending up one of our own to change it because there was always another nut with another gun, probably fronting some government conspiracy. Best to just turn away, turn up the record player, get back to the party, and write the whole political circus off as an outdated system that really didn't affect us.

The day George Wallace got shot, I felt the same sad, disgusted anger knot around my stomach. I never agreed with a single thing Wallace said, yet the day he was shot, I felt a deep sorrow for our society and a fear for the future of a nation that used guns to make points. The fact that bullets could rip open conservatives as easily as they could liberals was of no comfort at all.

And the shooters weren't quite done yet.

For me, and I suspect for some others about my age, a new day has supplanted JFK's assassination as "the day everyone remembers what they were doing."

I was backing my car out of the driveway at my wife's parents' house when I heard on the car radio that John Lennon had been shot.

My first response was to be absolutely stunned, as though I'd been walking with my head down and walked into a wall.

Then I thought it might be a prank. It hadn't been that long since the rainy day when my friend Jim and I were riding in his car and heard on the radio that Paul McCartney was dead.

The announcer repeated the news about John and the Dakota and the bullets, and I could tell by his voice it was true.

The words landed hard, as though the opening chord of "Hard Day's Night" had been played on an out-of-tune guitar.

All of us Beatles fans believed it was only a matter of time before the boys got back together and recorded another album. They were having a spat, they would get over it, and they would show us the way once again. We figured there was nothing—not bickering wives, not Beatles' egos, not Wings—that would keep that from happening.

We didn't consider a sick kid with a gun.

When I was a teenager, I used to wake up every morning and wonder what the Beatles were doing that day. They were gods who walked the earth. It never occurred to me that one of them could die.

I was on my way to my job, as night manager of a restaurant, the day John was killed. When I got there, the owner asked me how I was doing.

"Not real good," I said.

"How come?"

"Didn't you hear the news?" I asked. "John Lennon got killed."

"Yeah...so what?"

All of my anger at the sick kid with the gun, at the FBI for trying to throw John out of America, at every kid in a blue Future Farmers of America jacket who ever made fun of my hair, was suddenly directed at him.

But I didn't act on it.

I needed that job.

A working class hero is something to be.

In his death, John Lennon reinforced his message of the senselessness of violence. I'm sure he would rather have skipped that lesson, though, and stuck around to watch Sean grow up.

It's one of the sorrows of my generation that we'll never know how history might have been different if JFK or Bobby or Martin or John had lived. Maybe their best years were behind them. Maybe they would have just chipped away at their own reputations. Or possibly there would have been still greater things they would have accomplished.

At least they could have watched their children grow.

I have tried to find some meaning in all of this, with the wisdom of my 50 years. I can't. The shootings seemed stupid then, and they seem stupid now.

So I stood for a time at Bobby Kennedy's gravesite, where the ripples move across a memorial fountain, one replacing anoth-er, forever.

If only we could replace human beings so easily.

FACING THE WALL

I'm sorry, James.

I apologize, David.

Forgive me, Dwight and Julio and Samuel and all 58,000 of your brothers whose names are carved beside yours in the rock.

I made a terrible mistake, and I'm sorry.

There are places I look forward to visiting when I come to Washington, D.C., and places I force myself to visit. I come to the Vietnam Veterans' Memorial because I have to.

The first knot in my stomach hits when I crest the hill on the path that winds through lovely, peaceful woods. I see the Wall for the first time then, in the distance, through trees. There are people in front of it, moving slowly, quietly, as if weighed down by their hearts.

Farther down the path, past the statue of three soldiers, I approach the first name. I am nervous. Afraid. I don't know why. I walk past name after name after name until they blend together into an enormous sorrow.

Ahead I see a woman on her knees, moving the edge of a pencil across paper to make a rubbing of the name underneath. It reminds me that each of these names was a person with a life and a family and a favorite TV show and a dream for the future.

Just like me.

My eyes mist over as I walk past more names.

I can't imagine what it must be like for someone who fought in Vietnam to visit this wall. I think it must take more courage than I have.

I was on the other side.

My friends and I thought the Vietnam War was a mistake, and we said so. I believed the Vietnam War was wrong because I believed all wars were wrong.

I don't apologize for that.

I am sorry, though, that the protests of so many of my generation were so misdirected. We had no right to mock or demonize the soldiers on the ground in Vietnam.

I suspect that the men fighting and dying in the jungles of Vietnam fell into one of two groups: those who would do anything their country asked of them because they believed in her leaders and her causes; and those who felt a lot like I did, except they wound up in Vietnam through fate or bad luck. Sometimes, when you're 19, you have no clue how to take charge of destiny, so you let the winds of fate carry you where they will.

We shouldn't have blamed the first group for being patriotic, and we shouldn't have blamed the second group for being unlucky.

But we did both enthusiastically.

There is a revisionist history going around now that claims war protests in the 1960s and early 1970s were never against foot soldiers, but against the masters of war who ran things.

Sorry. I wish that were true.

Members of my generation, protesting for the power rush and sheer joy of it, weren't that careful when we chose our targets. We needed to shout at someone, so we shouted at anyone in uniform. Never mind that the uniform was on someone our older siblings went to high school with. Never mind that the skinny private with the shaved head would rather have been wearing bell-bottoms and bangs. Never mind that he walked with a limp now, or seemed to have more trouble concentrating than when he left. The uniform made him fair game.

The most strident of us spat on soldiers, or cursed them, or laughed at them, or called them fools.

Those less courageously vocal, like I was, saw anyone in any uniform as the enemy and, therefore, the enablers of war.

One of the early pop songs to protest the Vietnam War was Donovan's "Universal Soldier," written by Buffy St. Marie. I remembered it fondly, and for years it was on my list of songs I wanted to have on tape again. When I finally found a copy, one line I had forgotten startled me.

"He's the universal soldier, and he really is to blame…"

There it was. I hadn't remembered how quick we all were to blame Vietnam on kids with guns.

Boys just a few years older than I were dying on the bottom of the world, and I was in my warm living room singing with Country Joe and the Fish.

"Be the first one on your block to have your boy come home in a box."

I remember that with shame, 35 years later, staring at the Wall.

So much of the great national debate about the war was misunderstanding each other's messages.

When we said "Give Peace a Chance," we weren't talking to America, but to the world. Our side, their side, everybody. To us, with our 12 or 14 or 18 years of life experience, it was so simple. Just don't fight wars. Just put down the guns. We're not savages anymore. We can work it out.

Barry McGuire summed it up in "Eve of Destruction," another early antiwar song.

"You don't believe in war? Then what's that gun you're totin'?"

And when we said those things, they thought we were saying "Give up! Let the other side win! Be cowards!"

So they said "America: Love It or Leave It!" and meant that there was a way things had always been in this country, a good way, a right way, and a way worth fighting to keep.

And we just thought they were blind followers of silly, outdated policies.

It was easier to shout at each other than to talk to each other. When you're a kid, shouting is just more fun, and when you're an adult, sometimes it's all you know.

So both sides dug in. And 19-year-old kids, listening in dark rain for footsteps in the jungle, got caught in the middle.

At my 30th high school reunion a few years ago, I got reacquainted with a former classmate who reminded me of an incident I'd forgotten. When he and I were 18, the Army recruiters came and got us and took us to the city for the weekend. We got free meals, a hotel room, and even went out to see a dirty movie, all on Uncle Sam. They wanted 18-year-olds to enlist, and they weren't above a little low-level bribery.

I had no intention of signing up, of course. It was just a big joke.

The other guy went to Vietnam.

In so many ways, he and I were the same guy. Except he went, and I didn't. Talking with him, laughing, and joking about that goofy weekend 35 years earlier, I realized that it wasn't about us and them. It was about us and us.

I have been sitting here for an hour, looking toward the Wall, and the line of people has never stopped. This is Monday morning, but it could be Sunday afternoon or Saturday night, and there would still be visitors at the Wall.

Clearly, this is something we're all still trying to come to terms with.

Each of those visitors has his or her own private thoughts while reading the names on the Wall. Here's mine—Did one of you go in my place?

EARLY AFTERNOON DELIGHT

Last time I lunched at Clyde's of Georgetown, I had the finest cheese-scrambled eggs I've ever had.

So that should tell you how long ago it was. Cheese and eggs have both been on my verboten list for quite some time now.

Clyde's is where Bill Danoff saw a menu item called "Afternoon Delight," then went home and wrote a song about it to record with his group, the Starland Vocal Band.

So as I sat in the brick courtyard with the sun warming through the skylight, that song kept running through my head. I didn't mind, since I seem to be one of the few people on earth who actually likes it.

I ate those cheese-scrambled eggs in the dark days of the latter 1970s. Those of us with guitars in our hands and protest songs in our hearts were fighting the good fight against disco.

One place we did that was at a bar just up the street from Clyde's. The bar was originally called "Rocky Raccoon's." The owner changed the name to something else, but that name has disappeared down a hole in the Sea of Holes that is now my memory.

The owner of whatever Rocky Raccoon's became used to hire me as an opening act for bands. It's a lot less showbiz than it sounds.

What it meant is that he'd call me about 4:30 in the afternoon to ask if I could open for some band that evening. I'd play for half an hour while people who had been drinking heavily waited for the band they'd paid to see. Often they would suggest that my time might be better spent elsewhere. When the half-hour ended, the owner would pay me 15 bucks.

One night I was opening for a blues band called the Nighthawks and, in the middle of a song, my guitar strap snapped. I made one of the most uncoordinated moves since Cro-Magnons slouched the earth in an attempt to catch the guitar. I missed, and it fell to the stage with a twangy, reverberating crash.

The crowd, which had been beerily conversing while completely ignoring me, fell dead silent, like an old West saloon when the bad guy walks in.

It was one of the two most humiliating experiences of my life, and if you think I'm going to tell you the other one, you must be loopy from the fumes.

So anyway, after lunch I walked up to where Rocky Raccoon's used to be.

I can't swear to it—memory holes, you know—but I think it's now the Ukrainian embassy. I hope so because that is so cool. Also, it would mean the famous Cellar Door folk music club across the street is now something called The Philadelphia Cheese Company.

Bill Danoff used to sing with John Denver at the Cellar Door. People thought John Denver was kind of cheesy. See how this is all coming together?

The other folk music club in Georgetown when I lived in these parts was Singer's Studio. It was a great venue, with such perfect acoustics that nobody used microphones.

One night all of the members of my therapy group came to

hear me perform there. It was the '70s. We all had therapy groups then.

Singer's Studio was a nonprofit, run by a guy who played nylon-string guitar and knew a whole lot of Edith Piaf songs in French. He got on my bad side by saying that most of my songs had the same melody, which was true, but I thought it rude of him to point it out.

Singer's Studio is also where I came in third at a songwriters contest. The same guy came in first and second. My songs were better than his, except for the melodies.

I hate songwriters' contests.

There was a street I used to walk down from Georgetown to get to Dupont Circle, near where I used to live. Just for fun, I thought I'd try to remember which street it was without asking any natives.

Apparently they ran out of good names while naming Washington streets because a lot of them are just named after letters. Probably it was late on a Friday afternoon, and they still had 26 streets to name before they could go home.

I decided the one I wanted was P Street and took off walking down its attractive brick sidewalks, in the shade of sheltering trees.

After a while, P Street seemed wrong, so I went down to O Street, which seemed better. A guy was walking his dog on O Street, and they both seemed friendly.

"Say, is this the street that goes right into Dupont Circle?" I asked. "One street up," he replied. "P Street."

Trust the force, Luke.

I had the turkey burger for lunch at Clyde's. Darned if it wasn't the best I've ever had.

SiX MiLLiON HEARTS

Vacant deep-socket eyes, whispering, begging, pleading.

Sick skin stretched tight over thin bone until it looks like leather. Like the leather in the shoes. Those thousands of shoes that were saved after the people who wore them were killed and burned.

Images so horrific as to make the devil turn away in disgust.

The Holocaust happened.

In the great span of time since humans have been here, 60 years is a heartbeat. Sixty years is yesterday. Sixty years is nothing.

The Holocaust happened yesterday. A heartbeat ago.

If you think it's ancient history and that we are too far advanced for it to ever happen again, you're wrong.

I followed a large crowd of high school students through the three floors of the permanent exhibit at the Holocaust Memorial in Washington. They talked among themselves and pointed at the pictures of bodies, the video clips of Hitler, and the wooden bunks.

Then one would stop and begin to write on the fill-in-the-blank sheet they all carried, and a crowd would gather round, copying whatever the first person was writing.

They were polite and respectful. No one giggled. But their goal was quite obviously to fill in those blanks.

I caught myself hoping that some of what they were seeing

would stick, that they would remember long after they had turned in the completed assignment.

It's the same way I hope my son will remember when I bring him here sometime after his 11th birthday, the age the museum suggests for viewing the permanent exhibit.

I want him to know the depths to which humans can sink, as well as the heights to which we can soar. I want him to see what people just like us did to people just like us, not very long ago.

They give you a little notebook at the beginning of your tour of the Holocaust exhibit. It has the name of a real person who was affected by the Holocaust on the cover, and you read it a bit at a time as you tour the exhibit. At the end, you find out how it ended for this one person.

My card was for Josef, who died at age 18 trying to blow a hole into the wall surrounding the Warsaw ghetto. Last time I came to this exhibit, my identification card was for a man killed in the camps because he was homosexual.

These little life-and-death stories have a powerful effect on me. There are people in my life who are 18 years old or homosexual or Jewish. I see their faces in these cards.

The Holocaust Memorial saddens me and angers me and frustrates me and scares me. I'll probably have nightmares about my visit here, just like last time.

But I will always come here when I come to Washington.

I need to be reminded of how recently prejudice was a wildfire that burned out of control and how easily it could happen again.

And I need to reexamine myself to make sure I'm still fighting that.

Prejudice is so insidious. Prejudice is rats nibbling around the corners of the door. It's a smiling demon that nudges you and urges you and entices you to join in ways so small as to be almost imperceptible.

None of us would take part in another Holocaust. The demon knows that. But maybe we would admit, just among our own kind, mind you, that our race or our religion or our nationality was just a little superior to another?

Not even that?

OK then, maybe we would apply some trait, any harmless little trait, to a group of people. All blacks are this. All Jews are that. All poor people are thus-and-so. If only women weren't so, oh, you know.

Not yet?

OK, then, let's make it a positive trait. They're great at sports. They're really smart. They sure are good to their moms.

And it's just as easy as that. We nod in agreement because, after all, we're all friends here.

And the demon wins one.

A small step, leading down a long road that ends where none of us want to be.

I've heard many times that as we age we become more conservative, and I know it's been true in my case. I've put aside a lot of my fierce liberal beliefs in the face of day-to-day existence. But on this one thing, I won't change.

I will believe until the day I die that we are all equal, and because of that, we should treat each other with respect.

The Holocaust Memorial reminds me to keep trying because it shows me what can happen if we don't.

POSITIVELY PENNSYLVANIA AVENUE

As a lifelong president-watcher, it pains me to say that I have no memories of Dwight D. Eisenhower.

I know who Ike was and what he did, of course, but I have no real memories of him. Not one. Even though he was president of the United States for the first seven and a half years of my life.

It's almost as though I had no interest in politics at all before I turned eight.

The number of presidents boomers have lived through keeps increasing, like the gray hairs on our heads or the reasons why we will wait until next year to run that marathon.

When we sort of elected George W. Bush in 2000, that made 10 presidents I've had the opportunity to like, dislike, or try to just ignore. The thing they had in common was that they were all fun to watch.

John F. Kennedy is the first president I remember, but then, getting murdered in office is a very memorable thing to a kid.

John Kennedy had wrought a tremendous change in the presidency because of his age and his attitude. To me it mostly meant that, rather than be like my grandfather, the president was now like a funny uncle.

One of the earliest memories I have of Kennedy is a song that was on the radio by a mimic who called herself Little Caroline and sang, "My daddy is president. What does your daddy do?"

My other memory might not be real. I've read so much about the Cuban missile crisis that I may have just made up a memory to go along with it. But I'm pretty sure I remember having the snowy TV program on our black and white set interrupted so the president could speak, then show jets on a runway, engines running, ready to bomb Cuba.

Except he called it "Cuber." I'm surprised he didn't call them "nucular" weapons.

I was in sixth grade when JFK died. In my 11th year, Lyndon Johnson became president.

I've since learned that Johnson did great things to fight the blood-deep racism in this country and to help the poor. His vision for a Great Society actually could have been pretty great if it had worked.

But that's not what I remember from that time. When I think about Lyndon Johnson, I always think about Vietnam. My friends and I, racing hairlong into our teenage years, always blamed LBJ personally for the Vietnam War.

I feel bad about that now, but at the time it seemed appropriate.

Johnson was a big goofy cowboy, and we of the Love Generation were more than happy to hang the war around his neck like a big "Kick Me" sign.

He came to us with his "heavy hort," and we shredded it.

America's youth were feeling their brown rice in the '60s and were in no mood to respect the president just because he was the president. That, in fact, seemed a good reason to prove we didn't have to respect him.

The 1960s had officially become "The Sixties." We were out to change the world, and those who wouldn't lend a hand needed to get out of the way.

So Country Joe and the Fish sang "Ode to a High-Flying Bird" and told LBJ to go back to Texas and work on his ranch. Johnson lifted his shirt to show off his surgery scar, and *Mad* magazine turned it into a map of Vietnam.

We helped drive LBJ out of office and were punished with Richard Nixon.

Nixon was elected when I was 16, and what I remember about that autumn is that I didn't care. My life existed in a small section of Pennsylvania and New York state and, as far as I could see, what those fools in Washington were doing didn't affect it much.

People my age and a bit older had already reached the unspoken conclusion that the stalled car that society had become could no longer be repaired and would, instead, have to be replaced.

Fortunately, we were up to the job, and we had a plan: Give peace a chance. All you need is love. Everybody get together.

Nixon was easy to dislike. His smile never reached his eyes. Sweat puddled on his upper lip when he shaded the truth, which was often. He kept using the two-fingered "V" sign to mean victory, seeming unaware that we were all using it to mean "peace."

Oh, he tried to be hip. He went on *Laugh-In* and said "Sock it to me?" and we laughed, not because it was funny, but because he thought doing it might make young people like him more. We laughed at him for thinking we were laughing with him.

Nixon always had the trapped-rat look of a guy who thinks everyone is out to get him. Turns out we were.

In the end, hoisted on the petard of Watergate, Nixon seemed genuinely surprised that we wanted him to give up the presidency just because he won it by cheating.

And he taught boomers a lesson that stuck for way too long:

All politicians were dishonest, and all politics was useless.

In the '60s we struggled through war, riots, marches, racial and social upheaval, generational distrust and discord, and the loss of faith in the leaders of our country.

Those things were exhausting.

No wonder by the early 1970s we were all ready to lay down our "Make Love, Not War" banners, stomp out the burning brassieres, and just get down and boogie!

Or, put another way, Jerry Ford became president.

I will always remember Jerry Ford fondly because of the great material he supplied to *Saturday Night Live* in its prime. Chevy Chase looked nothing like Ford, but when he fell across a podium and off the edge of the stage, there was no doubt whom he was parodying.

And I still use the line "alert Secret Service agents wrestled the fork to the ground." Too often, if you ask the people I keep using it on.

Ford was a good, honest, decent man, just the kind of guy we all loved to make fun of. Here was a guy who thought inflation could be whipped if we all just wore buttons. Like any good Midwestern dad, he threw up his hands and just admitted that his kids were beyond his control.

Jerry Ford was absolute proof that anyone really could grow up to be president. Anyone.

Which I guess opened the White House door for Jimmy Carter.

I really liked Jimmy Carter. He seemed to be the chosen one who could at last prove our point: A good man would be a better president than a good politician would.

I was 24 when Jimmy Carter was elected and, to people my age and a few years older, he seemed like the first president who really noticed us.

He brought rock and roll to the White House, for one thing. And a fresh, young staff of people with the knowing look of those who have partied at the frat house very recently. It seemed as though Carter wasn't just shushing us back to the kids' table so the grown-ups could talk.

Plus, he was so darn entertaining. He was a born-again Christian who talked to Playboy about lust, wore work shirts, had Willie Nelson over to the White House, and always listened to his mama.

And then, as if having that peanut-farmer accent and way too many teeth for his smile weren't precious enough, he had a brother who had his own beer named after him.

That, my friends, is entertainment!

Jimmy Carter had everything going for him except the fact that he wasn't a very good president. Doesn't mean he wasn't a fine man. Just not a fine president.

He's made a great ex-president, though. Best ever, in this, my book.

Too bad that he couldn't have just run for ex-president and skipped the pesky "being president first" part.

I lived in Washington, D.C., during the Carter years and left just before they elected Ronald Reagan. So, in a way, I blame myself.

My compatriots and I had made sport of Ronald Reagan for years. If I remember correctly, which I often don't, he was mentioned from the stage at Woodstock. One of the acts referred to him as "Ronald Ray-guns." We spoke irreverently about his hair and the dangers of a grease fire. We remembered when he was the host of *Death Valley Days,* and some of us had even seen *Bedtime for Bonzo* on TV.

So imagine our surprise when he actually became president, just as he endlessly said he would.

It seemed appropriate somehow that we had elected an actor president. By that time we had learned that presidents weren't the supermen we'd been taught they were when we were kids. So maybe if we couldn't elect our ideal, we could at least elect a trained actor to pretend he was.

The thing that surprises me about Ronald Reagan is the number of people out there who think he's the best president we ever had. Day after day they call the radio talk shows, willing to chip in for the dynamite to start blasting his image into Mount Rushmore.

Seems more to me like he was a harmless guy who could deliver a well-crafted line in a believable voice.

Of course, it's impossible to talk about Ronald Reagan without mentioning the tragic hand fate dealt him in the final years of his life. In one of history's great sad ironies, the one presidential couple who seemed most likely to live the fairy tale happily-ever-after dream together were robbed of the chance by dreadful disease.

It's always nice to have the vice president follow the president into the White House. For one thing, it cuts way down on moving expenses. And so, we elected Reagan's preppie veep.

OK, so George Bush wasn't exactly a preppie. It was just fun to write "preppie veep."

Bush the elder did good things, of course. He got our boys out of Iraq. If not for him, we'd have never known Barbara. He kept Dana Carvey on TV and out of movies. He brought us the endlessly fascinating Dan Quayle.

His shortcoming, I think, was one not of his own making. He had the misfortune to be elected just after the enormously charismatic Ronald Reagan and just before the enormously charismatic Bill Clinton.

Bill Clinton—boomers finally were able to elect one of our own…a man who couldn't jog past a donut shop…a man who played bad saxophone at his own inauguration…a man who discussed undergarments on national television and in private conversations with young interns.

Well, what did we expect? Need I repeat—we elected one of us! You know us. You know what we're like. I mean, boomers are cool and everything, but most of us just aren't presidential material.

Bill Clinton was that guy you elect class president because you're pretty sure he'll sneak beer on the field trip bus.

I liked Clinton. Still do. I wanted to condemn him for having the audacity and lack of common sense to play "I spy a thong" with a girl young enough to be his daughter. And while I think that's a scummy thing for a husband and father to do, I don't think it made him a bad president. I've read some history books in the past 20 years, and I've learned that the man I think was the best president ever, FDR, had just about a watch-pocket full of morals. Didn't make him a bad president.

No, I think Clinton's problem was one of goals. He spent his whole life wanting to become president until, by Hillary, he did. He just didn't seem to have a clear idea of what he should do then.

We hiked him the football, and he held onto it while he flirted with the cheerleaders.

And yet, we are ever hopeful. When it came time to replace him, we eliminated all the wanna-be-presidents until the only candidates left spending were a couple more yuppie boomers.

If a crystal ball gazer had told me when I was a kid that I'd live through two presidents with the same last name, I wouldn't have been surprised. I just thought the name would be "Kennedy."

September 11th gave George W. Bush a daunting task to perform. Stopping terrorists is like fighting bees. No matter how many you manage to swat, there's always another one waiting to sting. Having said that, I don't see how caging the dog because the cat pees on the carpet was supposed to help.

I've been watching presidents now for most of my life, with hope, with disgust, with disbelief, with pride. Along the way, I've realized that they may package themselves as perfect for the presidency, but really, nobody's perfect for anything. America was wrong to pretend that presidents are somehow better than the rest of us. They are the rest of us. The best we can hope for is that they're decent folks who work hard and do their best, and that their best is good enough.

Most of the ones I've lived through so far have been exactly that.

But I'm sad that, as a voter, I have so little to say about who gets to sit in the White House. I get to choose between the two people who have played the money game well enough to become candidates, and sometimes it's a rate-a-record match between two tunes you can't dance to.

Still, I keep voting. It seems important to get up early and wait in that long line. It seems worth it even though, for the past 20 years, my wife and I have cancelled out each other's vote every Election Day.

Our son is nearly 10 now. The next president may be the first one he remembers.

(AUTHOR'S NOTE: This book went to press before the results of the 2004 election were known.)

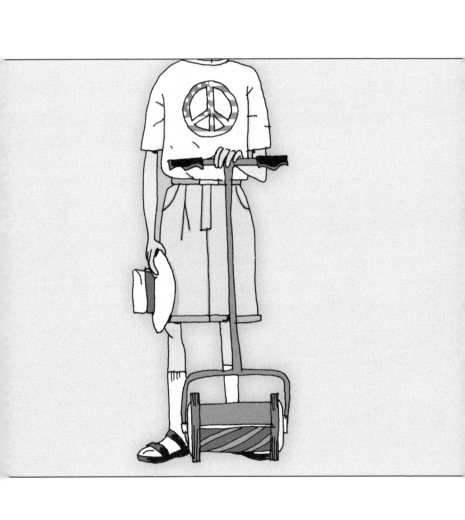

OLD HiPPiES NEVER DiE

I used to think 50 was old. Turns out that's just one of the many things I had wrong. My new motto: Do not go gently into midlife.

BOOM, BABY, BOOM

There are 76 million baby boomers, give or take a boom.

That's somewhere over a billion pounds of wobbling flesh, if you count the 760 million pounds we lost last year and the 758 million we gained back at the holidays.

We are a divergent group. Indeed, one of the few things we have in common is the years we were born.

Technically, boomers were born between 1946 and 1964.

The oldest boomers are war babies—born during Benny Goodman, in their teens during Elvis, in college with the Beatles.

The youngest were born during the "British Invasion" and were teenagers during the disco years. May God have mercy on their souls.

I am comfortably ensconced right in the middle of this large, noisy, insistent generation. I was born during the Korean War, grew up during the Vietnam War, and am still around during the war on terrorism.

So a bunch of boomers have already turned 50. You may not have noticed, since they weren't as whiney about it as I.

Many of us rebel against the term "baby boomer" since, well, it's a label, man. We don't need no stinkin' labels. As with most labels, it assumes that we're similar when we're really not. I'm not even similar to myself about half the time.

Boomers are liberal and conservative, married and single, Christian and atheist, straight and gay, Democrat and Republican, short and tall, athletic and me. Just try to get a bunch of us to agree on a restaurant sometime.

Still, there may be things we have in common.

For one, we seem to be reluctant to get out of the way for the next generation.

In my father's day—and certainly my grandfather's—it was expected that a person would put in his time on the job, then retire and move aside so the younger folks with the fancy college degrees could take over.

It was an understanding that went beyond occupations. There was a natural passing of the torch. Our parents and grandparents may not have liked getting older and becoming less of a force of the nature of things, but they did it because it was what people did. At some point, they stopped trying to change the world and accepted the reality that the world was going to change, and probably in ways they wouldn't agree with. My people aren't having any of that. We may have no choice but to get older, but that doesn't mean we have to look older or act older.

In the past few days, I've read two articles in my "morning coffee" paper about boomers.

The first was about tooth implants.

That's right, operator…tooth implants.

Now, instead of the false teeth of our fathers and mothers, we can all have permanent teeth implanted in our jawbones. We'll eat apples and never whistle an "S." We'll never have to explain the glass on the nightstand to a date. Again, we have found a way around paying the toll on Route Over-50.

The implants cost a lot more than false teeth, which makes

the implants even more attractive to boomers. We have more money than we've ever had, and we see no finer place to spend it than on ourselves. Can you say "Botox"?

The second article was about how boomers are demanding new ways to treat the aches and pains associated with aging.

It was for past generations to gracefully accept the aching feet and backs that come with a lifetime of walking and bending, and slow down accordingly. Not for us, thank you.

If we tell our doctors it hurts when we do that, they darn well better not try to tell us not to do that. We intend to keep our bicycles, tennis rackets, skis, and jogging shoes. We'll be at the beach no matter how bad we look in the suits. There are lots of doctors out there, and we can still get around plenty well enough to find a new one.

We don't like pain. And when we don't like things, we don't accept them. Stow the stoicism, we say. Bring on the pinball wizard with the miracle cure.

I think we keep biking and running and swimming and skiing mostly because those things are fun, and because we have promised ourselves that we won't be dads and moms who sit on the deck and smoke while our kids play.

But I wonder, don't we also stay active so we can tell those who would usurp us to keep their low-rider pants on? It's not time yet. When our parents were our age, it may have been time for them to stand aside and let someone younger ride in the front roller coaster car. We're not our parents.

You're not dealing with a bunch of Aunt Bea's, humming in the kitchen while Andy runs Mayberry.

Gee. Look at me, will you? Committing the cardinal sin. After all my big talk, here I am lumping us all together, saying that all boomers feel the same way.

Of course, that's not the case. You'll find lots of boomers who want nothing more than to sit on the sofa and knit while the grandchildren play, or fall asleep in the recliner in front of the football game.

But the important thing to keep in mind is they do those things because they want to and because they can, not because anybody said they were supposed to. It has nothing to do with the roles society has given to people over 50 in the past. Those days are as gone as clacker balls and P.F. Flyers.

If you find us in our rocking chairs with a book, it's because we feel like sitting in our rockers and reading for a while. Don't let that give you any ideas about putting our in-line skates in the garage sale box.

We'll let you know when we're done.

THERE IS A TIME...TURN TURN TURN

I know, I've said I won't go gently into midlife. But I will enter this new context with a different set of perceptions, perspectives, priorities than I ever thought I'd have back in my hippie years.

＊　　＊　　＊　　＊　　＊

There is a time for change…always.

Take the vacation I'm on with my family as I write this.

My family didn't take vacations when I was a kid. My brothers and sisters and I spent a week at our grandparents' house each summer, where we filled the days swimming in the creek, listening to hot rod songs and scavenging for golf balls from the nearby course. In the evening we would have supper featuring Grandma's pies, baked from scratch using the fruit she had canned the previous harvest season. Then I'd snuggle next to Grandpa in the creaky rocking chair, which he had made from scratch using leftover wood. Before *Bonanza* ended, I'd drift off to sleep to the smell of Old Spice aftershave and Prince Albert pipe tobacco.

Dad worked at his job 50 weeks a year, then during his two weeks of vacation, he worked for my uncle, tossing leaden hay bales shoulder-high onto a truck.

So, I don't have any stories about great family vacations or disastrous family vacations. The wife and I have decided this won't happen to our son. We take him on vacations so he'll have lots of stories someday.

There. Did you see what I just did there?

I made it clear that the reason we go on vacation is for our son. Not for me.

There is still too much of my father rattling around in me to say that I take vacations for fun. No, they are just another one of the fatherly duties I must perform. Poor, pitiful me.

Over the years I have excised many of the personality traits I got through osmosis from my dad, but that one sticks. Judging by the dads I observe while on vacation, it's like that for a lot of guys my age.

We compensate in many ways for not being at work where we belong. We grumble about four-dollar hot dogs. We drive rental cars on unfamiliar one-way streets. We carry our bags through airports instead of rolling them on their built-in wheels. We read amusement park guidebooks and make out daily itineraries. We get antsy and short-tempered when the family doesn't follow our daily itineraries. We write essays on airplanes while everyone else is staring out the window at the Rockies.

An ironic thing is that the family trip we're on as I write this is more of a vacation for me than it is for my wife. She has a business meeting at the hotel. My son and I are just tagging along.

There. See? Did it again. We're not really taking a vacation. It's a necessary trip for one of us. Any fun we have will be strictly coincidental.

I always figured I knew why stereotypical retired people travel so much. They have the time, I thought. They don't have kids to raise. They have more money.

Lately I'm starting to think that retired guys travel a lot for one other reason. Maybe they finally get over their guilt about taking better vacations than their fathers did.

At least I hope so. I can see retirement up ahead, just over the horizon. And look…the sun seems to be setting on a beach. And there's a guy there, and he's…he's…relaxing!

And there's not a hay bale in sight.

*   *   *   *   *

There is a time for renewal…

For me, that time is now. I need to let my young son reintroduce me to a world of excitement, joy, beauty, one where everything is an adventure of discovery and wonder.

The waves sweep in to love-pat the shore, bubbling up on warm sand, only to be pulled back by the gravity of an unseen smirking moon.

Yo-ho, the mysterious siren call of the sea. My son hears it.

I can't hear it.

Did I mention the waves crashing in and going back out? Over and over and over? I did? Because that's about all you get with the sea.

Yes, there are craggy rocks and glistening sand. And there's that great blue nothing out toward the edge of the world. But that's about all. It's all very beautiful, of course, as nature always is.

But if it's calling me, my line's busy.

My grandfather answered the call of the sea. He ran away from home and lied about his age to join the Navy.

The sea called some of his sons, too, and today it's calling mine.

That's why I pace the beach, craning my neck like a gray seagull, trying not to be overprotective as my boy wades out into the ice-water Pacific.

He holds up his latest trophy.

"Look, Dad! A seashell!"

"Cool!" I shout, all the while thinking "Undertow! Undertow! Undertow!"

My son has always been better at joy than I.

When he was in first grade, he could ride his bike to school if a parent rode along with him. Sometimes I was that parent. There was a steep hill on the way, and when he went down it, he would shout a loud, sustained "Wooo-hooo!" as though there was so much joy inside him that it had to come out as a holler.

I feel like that when the wheels of a plane leave the ground. But I don't shout. In these strange days, that might cause a panic. Plus, I'm a grown-up.

Sometimes being a grown-up is a fine thing. It got me in to see *Die Hard* without a parent or guardian, and afterward I didn't have to wait for my dad to come and pick me up.

Still, on a cold day at Sea World, my son didn't hesitate to sit in the splash zone at the whale show. I moved back a few rows, claiming to protect the cameras.

While his mom and I grumbled and schlepped bags down the hall of the interminable airport terminal, he was spinning his backpack on wheels around himself in circles, singing.

His life motto seems to be that of most kids: "Let's make this interesting!"

He's coming out of the cold saltwater now. He's made a new friend—another thing he's better at than I am—and they're heading down the beach to look for sand crabs.

I follow behind, with the towels and shoes and hooded sweatshirt, down the beach in front of the Hotel Del Coronado, where Tony Curtis flirted with Marilyn Monroe in *Some Like It Hot*.

Sorry, Tony. Today I'm more envious of a certain little boy.

*   *   *   *   *

There is a time for hope…

When I was a kid I pretended clothespins were soldiers because I didn't have molded plastic army men.

I thought about this while watching my son, on an airplane headed for the ocean, playing his Game Boy.

This is his third plane trip and his second ocean.

Because he shares his mother's love of animals and nature, and has added his own love of science, we paid extra so he could swim with dolphins.

I don't think he's an unusually pampered child, judging by the kids he plays with and the things they have.

When I was a kid and would complain about what the other kids had and I didn't, my dad would tell me about the Depression, when he ate grass soup.

Then he'd tell me I didn't know how lucky I was.

He was right.

I hope my son doesn't know how lucky he is, either. I hope he is able to just accept that life is full of great things.

K-9 DU JOUR

I don't mean to go all "Travels with Charley" on you, especially since I am to Steinbeck as the dirt clod that falls from my shoes after a run is to Pikes Peak. Still, it may interest you to know that our big, goofy black lab, JJ, has been involved in these writings.

That may explain a lot.

While I've been typing, misspelling, grumbling, deleting, and retyping, he's been sleeping nearby. It's not until I eventually get the germ of a good idea that he will interrupt me in mid-thought by clawing at the patio door to go out. Once outside, he'll turn around and scratch the door to come back in. For this he expects some sort of treat.

JJ would make a good employee for a major corporation.

We have JJ because my wife and son are huge animal lovers. Yes, they love huge animals. They love small animals too. My wife will spend 50 dollars for surgery on a three-dollar hamster. It's one of the things I love about her. There are others.

So I share my home with a dog, continuing a lifelong trend.

Dogs were as much a part of my childhood as trees or bikes or scabs.

They were good, sturdy, no-nonsense '50s dogs that slept outdoors and ate table scraps. The creek was their bathtub, the porch their umbrella, and the world their toilet.

Theoretically, they were working dogs.

My uncle had a collie named Lassie. Already you know a lot about my uncle.

Lassie was a Border collie without a border. He made do by chasing bored cows around and around pastures, then cantering into the barn to plop exhausted on the hay.

And one day—nobody really knew how—he became our dog.

I can think only of one time that I purposefully got a dog. I was nine. He was an unholy mix of breeds that my father assumed would be a hunting dog. Mostly he hunted dropped hot dogs at family cookouts.

We called him Tank, which seemed to suit him.

We kept these dogs around because they weren't much trouble, they seemed to like us, and it was easier than getting rid of them.

When it came their time to go, we let them go. Sometimes our father helped them along a little.

A lot of the pretend-hippies I knew in the 1960s had dogs, more as accouterments than companions. Often these dogs wore red bandannas, like hairy little four-legged cowboys.

I saw a lot of them when I went to college. Apparently, you could major in Frisbee if you had a dog, judging by the amount of time a lot of the other students spent tossing plastic flying discs to their dogs on the quad.

The dogs often went to class, wearing saddlebags full of their owners' books, which I just thought was rude. Just because you're stuck in Psych 101 on the first warm spring day doesn't mean your dog should suffer.

As one of the last gasps of the dying 1960s, the college passed a rule saying dogs could no longer come to class. Students who couldn't have cared less about the Pentagon Papers or Watergate were ready to wage war over this assault on their freedom.

Petitions circulated around campus. Students may have boy-cotted classes, although it was sometimes hard to tell.

After the passion subsided, there was a new common sight on campus: Dogs in red bandannas and saddlebags, waiting patiently outside classrooms.

We acquired JJ because our previous dog, KC, died. Don't ask about the initial thing.

In the early days of our marriage my wife came home with KC, a Yorkshire terrier. She had made a special trip, chosen the dog with loving care, and cradled it in her lap all the way to our apartment. She heaped attention and love on the dog, and, in return, KC immediately decided that she was really my dog. She stretched out alongside my leg on the couch while I watched TV and snuggled against my back while I slept. Before long I was one of those guys you see driving down the street with a little dog standing on his lap, panting at the driver's side window.

So I had to stop making fun of those guys.

A lifetime of sharing homes with dogs has taught me that if a dog adopts you, obedience school's out, pal. You might as well just relax and let the river flow, and hope the river isn't yellow and flowing on your carpet.

Our pets tend to be misfits.

KC, for example, was bald. Not on her head, but in a stripe all the way down her back. We gave a lot of money to vets to try to correct the problem and eventually just learned to live with it. So, while other people with Yorkies were greeted with "Oh, how precious!" the greeting we got was usually "What happened to your dog?" As though we had shaved her as a prank.

And now, JJ.

Here's the thing about Labrador retrievers: They make great dogs, but they make lousy puppies.

When my son was born, I was delighted to give up my selfish ways. I was in my 40s when he came along, and I was ready.

Can't finish the paper because Aaron needs to be fed? Cool!

Can't watch TV because he needs to be changed? Bring it on! We have to be really quiet so we don't wake him up? I can do that!

I had no such feelings for the infant JJ.

When he disrupted my sacred morning ritual—Cheerios with sliced peaches, comics page, 20 minutes of peace and quiet before everyone else gets up—I was not amused.

When he clamped his razor fangs on my toes in the middle of *ER,* I was less than accommodating.

Over and over I screamed, "All I ask is to watch one TV show! Is that too much to ask?" I hollered it, even though doing so made me sound just like my father.

Turns out that Lab puppies are the opposite of little boys. The dogs mellow out at age two.

JJ is my dog du jour. Acquired through no effort on my part, he is still, I have to admit, part of the family. When he comes around with his open face and sad eyes, letting me know that it's time for me to rub his neck, I feel really good about that.

Still, you won't get me to say I love him. "Love" is a word I reserve for people and Beatles songs.

But he's a good dog.

AND THEY WiLL KNOW US BY OUR ELBOWS

Summer's here again, and first-run TV is over for the season. This has driven the normally sofa-bound into the sunny outdoors. Kids are splashing in lawn sprinklers, and mosquitoes are tying on little "Soup's On! Come and Get It!" bibs.

As the summer days get longer, the summer pants get shorter. Arms go native in tank tops and sleeveless blouses. Swimming pools, lakes, and beaches call to us. Although sometimes the beaches just wave.

Those like me, teetering around the mid-century mark, gird ourselves to ungird ourselves for yet another season. We know all too well that the refreshing pool lies on the other side of a labyrinth in which the dreaded swimsuit monster lurks.

If the song is correct and you really do gotta be cruel to be kind, swimsuit designers must be kind beyond belief.

It's worse for women my age, of course. But then, pickup basketball is worse for men my age. These things even out in the end.

Sorry. Didn't mean to bring up ends when discussing swimsuits.

I often watch people whom I think are close to my age. It's restful. Also, I can compare my progress to theirs, and since I'm weighing the results, I always come out on top.

Sorry. I didn't mean to bring up tops when discussing swimsuits. Or weighing.

The vast majority of swimmers my age seem to have reached the "to heck with it" stage. There is very little sucking in of the guts or sitting in just the right position so the cellulite won't pucker. They are not about to stay in out of the fun just because their bodies aren't 16. If the perfect, hard, young folks don't like it, well, that's why God gave them shuttable eyelids and swivelly heads that can turn away.

This attitude seems especially prevalent among couples with kids or grandkids. They are so out of the game, they might as well turn in the cleats and hit the showers anyway.

The beachcombers I find a little more interesting are those baby boomers not in the majority. They are the ones trying to beat Father Time at his own wrinkly game. They work out. They stay buff. They buy this year's swimsuit, even though the one they bought four years ago is still good. From a distance, and when you're not wearing your glasses in the pool, they could be five or even ten years younger than they really are.

Often, they're wearing T-shirts.

I always thought it was only a matter of time before designers came out with a man's swimsuit with an attached shirt. We could all pretend we were wearing it because it was trendy, but we'd all know the real reason. I figured this would have happened by now because there are so many boomer guys who would pay twice as much for a suit like that.

I mean, was it really a coincidence that the bottom parts of some women's suits started to look like shorts again just when the boomers hit middle age? What would be so wrong in giving the guys a break by giving us a shirt?

It makes great sense to wear a T-shirt in the water. The sun is a dangerous seductress, especially to people who have spent many summers in her embrace. Why risk a bad belly burn when you can just wear the T-shirt?

If you believe that's why guys my age wear T-shirts in the pool, I have a used ab exerciser I'd like to sell you.

We're not wearing the wet T-shirts to relive our carefree college kegger days. Through haphazard workouts, some boomers have managed to stay in sort of OK shape. Except, of course, for the one pesky body part that just won't firm up or thin down. That's the one we think we're hiding with the T-shirt. I'm not about to rat out which body part it is. Let's just say that if we ever need to be rescued, the lifeguard will find convenient built-in handles with which to lift us out of the surf.

There is a third group of boomers beyond these two.

Some men and women our age actually have stayed in remarkable shape. I can't tell you exactly what the remarks about their shape are. Imagine a comic strip balloon full of punctuation marks.

You can often spot them by implants. Top of the head ones for men, a bit lower for the women. They are the women whose chests are constantly at attention, while the rest of their bodies are at ease.

I see them once in a while, the men smug and shirtless, the women haughty in bikinis, all daring you to guess their age, knowing you'd be wrong.

But I've noticed something when they walk away. No, not that.

In the natural motion of Homo sapiens walking, they bend their arms at the elbows, which stretches the skin. But as they keep walking, the arms straighten, and there it is—that ever-wrinkled, three-inch patch of skin on the back of each arm telling us and the world—you can run, but you can't hide.

Well, OK, you probably can't run as fast as you used to, either.

I've decided that elbow ironing must be an especially difficult plastic surgery. Even people with faces pulled so tight that blinking is but a memory still have the wrinkled elbows.

So go ahead, defiant ones. Wear the toupee. Color the gray blonde. Ripple the abs. Flex the pecs. Have the lard "Hoovered" out of your bottom half and pumped back into your top half.

Won't matter. The elbows don't lie.

Because of that, I'm thinking the swimsuit with attached shirt for guys also needs to have long sleeves.

i FOUGHT THE LAWN AND...

There comes a time in the life of every suburban homeowner when...

Wait a minute. I feel a digression coming on. When did I become a suburban homeowner? This wasn't supposed to happen.

OK, so I was never one of those who thought I'd wind up on a commune somewhere, growing my own brown rice and hitching rides on Wyatt's or Billy's motorcycle down to the swimming hole. I loved Snickers too much for that.

What I envisioned was more being the owner of a huge estate with gardeners and a full-time handyman. Not that I would care about the estate, of course, since it was a possession, and possessions were what I was imagining not having. Still, it's easier to imagine no possessions when you have some in the first place.

At the least I thought I'd live in a cool downtown loft, where my guitars would lean up against my Hollywood bed, the only piece of furniture I would need since I would never actually be there.

Instead, I find myself a suburban homeowner. And a digressing one at that.

Now, back to my point...

There comes a time in the life of every suburban homeowner when he or she considers a riding lawnmower.

For me, that time came yesterday.

It was the first time I've actually been called on to cut the grass on our big corner lot this growing season.

My wife, a perfect combination of porcelain beauty and hearty pioneer stock, has been doing a lot of the heavy lifting on our lawn this spring. We planted some new grass to cover the bald spots—it seemed easier than trying to comb over the grass that was already there—and the lawn has required constant watering. So while I was off gallivanting around, pretending to be a writer, my wife was hauling out several miles of kinky hose to water the tender, new blades.

She was also out there raking and planting a lot of the seed in the first place, all the while asking me questions that I pretended to know the answers to because, after all, I'd spent five minutes talking to the guy at the lawn and garden shop.

This was part of my never-ending quest to not be the cul-de-sac doofus. My goal when planting lawn seed is not to grow grass, just as my goal when applying weed killer is not to kill weeds. My goal when staining the deck is not to actually apply stain to the deck, and my goal when trimming back the tree limbs is not to trim back the tree limbs.

My goal in all of those things is not to look like a doink.

Just because I don't have a clue what I'm doing is no reason why people should think I don't have a clue what I'm doing. Can I help it if I was too busy learning the drum part to "Ticket To Ride" to pay attention while my dad was doing all the dad stuff he did so well?

It's vital for me, then, to do nothing that would give the neighbors cause to nod knowingly at each other and snicker. Those are not the kind of snickers I want.

Was I digressing again? Sorry.

The neighbor kid cut the grass once while I was gone. It grew back. Like the hair in my ears, it always grows back.

My turn.

Things went south on me right from the start. As soon as I began to grunt the mower up the first little hill, I felt something fly up under my shirt. I did what any self-respecting guy would do—yelped like a puppy and started slapping myself on the chest. Almost immediately the thing under my shirt stung me a third nipple.

I'm no entomologist, but I'm guessing it was something in the bee family. Specifically, a son of a bee.

As a bonus, my son, home sick from school, was chalk-drawing a Metabot court on our driveway and saw the whole, pitiful dance.

All of this left me in no mood for the two-hour plus job ahead.

It takes that long because I have a big lawn and a push mower. It's a gas mower, since our lawn is too expansive for the rotary-blade kind. But I did insist on one that didn't have motor-driven front wheels. You actually have to push it.

It was a pride thing.

My argument was that it didn't make sense for me to go to the gym five days a week—OK, four...usually—then spend the weekend riding round and round the lawn when I could be getting a good two-hour workout in the sunshine.

So I have grunted and sweated and sunburned for two hours, once a week, from April to October, for 10 years. It takes about a month of mowing before I stop waking the day after with a lawn hangover: sore back, sore neck, sore legs, bad attitude.

My argument for a push mower, originally a sound one, is starting to grow as thin as many sections of my lawn.

Yesterday, while cutting the dandelions, chickweed, clover, and occasional blades of grass, I came up with some new arguments.

The fact that I try to work out most days makes it perfectly acceptable for me to take it a little easy on weekends. I could use the time spent mowing for more valuable things. The sun is bad for me. This lawnmower is probably on its last wheels and will need to be replaced soon anyway. Some of those riding lawnmowers are pretty cool.

All of this may sound like just so much rationalization. There's a reason for that. It is just so much rationalization.

There's nothing wrong with rationalization. Rationalization is what helps people my age sleep with a clear conscience.

Assuming that we're not being kept awake by the backache we got from mowing the lawn.

FIDGETING ON A HOT STOVE

One of my mildly disgusting habits—I'll get to one of the others in a few paragraphs—is to reheat coffee in the microwave.

I can fairly hear coffee snobs all over town gasping and doing spit takes.

I don't make fresh coffee in the afternoon because, if I did, I would drink it all. So I pour the cold dregs from the morning pot into a mug and nuke it in the microwave.

While I was doing that today, I was reminded of something that people my age would prefer to never be reminded of.

As the microwave clock ticked down the seconds—7…6…5…4…it reminded me that my seconds are also ticking away. In the great microwave oven of life, it's just a matter of time before the beep signals that I'm done.

People of my generation are offended by this fact.

We've never been ones to accept the status quo, unless you mean the rock band. We want things our way, and we whine or cajole or insinuate ourselves into the decision-making process until we get things our way.

The rules that have always applied, we think, shouldn't apply to us. It was that way with the rules about haircuts, skirt lengths, lipstick colors, and relationships, and it should be that way with the rules about death.

We're not gonna take it.

And the gods look down and laugh that snorty laugh of theirs that many people think is distant thunder, but you and I know better.

We have been the victims of a cosmic prank, so complicated in its structure that it deserves its own room in the house of games.

It works like this:

We're all born knowing nothing and remain that way for the next 40 years. Around that time, we start to catch the tiniest glimpse of truth and begin to start figuring out a few of the things we've been struggling with for so long.

Over the next 10 years, we calm down a little. We start to see which cards are worth holding and which we should discard. We start—just start—to learn how we want to live.

And then it hits us. Learning how to better use our time has taken a whole lot of our time. We become better people every day, but fewer and fewer days remain for us to be better people.

Worse, we know this is a trend that will continue. I know more about life at 49 than I knew at 39. A decade of learning. It follows, then, that I'll know more at 60 than I do at 50. Among the things I'll know is how I could have better spent those 10 years. But they'll be gone, like grains of sand through a goose.

Our perfect self slows down over time so we can catch up, but when we finally do, it will be too late to do us any good.

It's as though we're given a grand piano at birth, and just when we're able to play something beyond "Heart and Soul," they repossess the piano.

When I first realized all of this, I developed a habit so annoying that even I'm annoyed by it.

When I'm reading the paper, and I read that someone famous has died, I check how old the person was and subtract my own age from it.

"Hmmm…that guy who used to be on that TV show was 77. That would give me 28 more years. So that would be 2030."

This works well for me if we're talking George Burns. Not so well with George Harrison.

I hate math. Still, since my son was born, I've added a second calculation.

"62 years old, huh? That would make my son 20."

I curse myself for waiting so long to have a child.

To see my son graduate from college, I have to make it at least to age 64. Another mental calculation I've done a couple of hundred times.

None of this is fun, and I would stop doing it if I could. I run the numbers now without even thinking. It's like sticking your tongue in the achy tooth.

I find myself wondering if the postulate "the better you become with time, the less time you have to be better" follows right through to its grand, ironic conclusion.

None of us can really know what the afterlife holds, but one thing I believe is that all of this will be made clear and that all of the big questions will be answered. In other words, I will know how to be my best self on the day after there is no time left.

As practical jokes go, that's way ahead of Prince Albert in the can.

We boomers find a number of ways to deal with the beckoning specter.

Denial is big. It explains why lots of us are in the gym or the plastic surgeon's office. We've put a lot of faith in our appearance over the decades. Maybe if we just keep looking young, Father Time will be fooled. Dads are so gullible.

It also explains why we call ourselves middle-aged, as though we expect to live to be 110. And why we say really silly things like "50 is still young."

Some boomers use the realization that they are as expendable as a *Star Trek* guest star to reexamine their faith.

It reminds me of a conversation I had with a preacher friend of mine when I was younger. He was detailing the tortures of hell for me when I interrupted him.

"Are you trying to scare me into being a Christian?" I asked.

And he replied, "Anything that works."

Turning 50 works.

When I was young I never thought about my own mortality. The young seldom do. In those days, I couldn't imagine a world without me in it.

Now, when I think about the time I've already had and the way I've used it, I would sometimes like a do-over.

I try not to wallow too deeply in that emotion. I don't think it helps to think about what we might have done differently. Clearly, it's better to concentrate on the banana smoothie still left in the blender, even if you can't see how much of it there is.

It helps me if I remember that the years spent fumbling and trying to figure things out weren't wasted. Just because I didn't know then what I know now, doesn't mean I didn't have a truckload of fun.

So, to the merry prankster that is time, I say, "Do your worst." Show me brief glimpses of the things that would have helped in the past.

If I learn a bit more every year about how to enjoy the moments, I figure the moments still left on the clock will be sweeter.

As Einstein is supposed to have said about relativity, there's a big difference between a minute spent looking at a pretty girl and a minute spent sitting on a hot stove.

So I will keep reminding myself of one important fact: Every minute I spend thinking about how many minutes I have left is a wasted minute.

STORE WARS

Every once in a while I'll take it in my head to do some crazy, nutty, goofy, insane thing for no apparent reason.

Like today, I went to a totally different grocery store.

I usually make the weekly grocery runs for our little three-some. It's not because I'm a fully liberated male, striving to erase unfair gender typing of household duties. Thanks for thinking that, though.

I buy the groceries because I am what my mom used to call a "picky eater."

My two brothers were also picky eaters. We earned the distinction by refusing to eat onions. Cooked or raw, red or sweet, Vidalia or whatever the non-Vidalia ones are called, it made no difference.

We lived a chili, spaghetti, and casserole-heavy existence, and it bugged my mom to no end that she had to serve those dishes bland and onionless.

My father cooked quite a bit, and he used onions. He liked onions. Used to eat them straight out of the garden. It made no difference to him that his boys didn't care for them. If he was layering the hamburger and sliced potatoes for shipwreck casserole, or kneading the rice, tomato paste and hamburger with his hands to create pigs in the blanket, in went the chopped onions.

It was up to my brothers and me to pick the onion bits out

and leave them in a pile on the outside edge of the plate.

Hence the term "picky eater."

I eat onions now, but I'm still a picky eater.

I want the bread made from crushed whole wheat, rather than the kind made from whole-wheat flour. I buy fat-free stuff, but not if the first listed ingredient is sugar or white flour. I don't want the bananas ripe, but just close enough to ripe so that they'll be edible both the following day and at the end of the week.

I would say I was anal retentive, except it's kind of a disgusting term to use in connection with food.

Even if you walk the supermarket tightrope and think you've gotten the foodstuffs I want, odds are I'll take something out of the grocery sack and wrinkle my prominent nose in displeasure.

So it's just better if I shop.

I have gone to the same grocery store for years, since that terrible day when they shut down the previous grocery store I had gone to for years.

I like patterns in my life. I appreciate sameness. If you throw me too many curves, I'm likely to call you a big cheater and take my bat and go home.

Recently, though, my grocery store has started to make me mad. They stopped carrying my bread, for example. I had to read the ingredients on every loaf of bread in the aisle to find it, and then one dark Saturday, it was gone.

I read an article that said kids were drinking too much bottled water, and they weren't getting enough fluoride. So I looked for the bottled water with added fluoride. They didn't have it. Never mind that soon afterward I read an article that said kids don't need the bottled water with fluoride, that they get plenty of fluoride without it. Maybe too much. Maybe what you should really give kids is an anti-fluoride bottled water.

My grocery store doesn't stock the most recent movie tie-in cereal that Aaron likes, either. And, as anyone who watches cartoons knows, that particular cereal is part of a balanced breakfast.

Obviously, I had to take some kind of action. Much as it might hurt both of us, I had to turn to another.

I like to think of myself as a considerate shopper, so I usually grab a cart from the parking lot on the way in. The carts were different at the new place. They were better, actually, but that's not my point here. They were different, which is to say, bad.

I felt a tingly rush as I entered the store proper, like a double-naught spy, undercover in a strange country.

Fruit comes first. Always has, always will. At my store, I crank a hard left toward the bananas and oranges. In this store, I had to turn to the right! Do you hear me? The right!

Salad stuff next. Dang! No prepackaged raw spinach! Gonna have to yank the stems off the leaves myself. They had the cherry tomatoes but no grape tomatoes. Oh well, I suppose I could cut them in half.

And so it went.

For the next 45 minutes, I found myself repeatedly looking at the shelf where something was supposed to be, only to find it two shelves lower and to the left. So the panic attack over not finding the canned peaches in light syrup where they were supposed to be was followed by the "Ha! Got'cha!" elation of locating them where they weren't supposed to be.

The new place didn't have the right bread, either. Or the fluoridated water I no longer needed. Or the little cheeseburger rice bowls my son likes.

They had the cartoon cereal, though, so that got them a

checkmark on the plus side.

When my long exploration of this strange planet was over, I went to the checkout.

"Do you have one of our Happy Shopper cards?" the lady with the bar code magic wand wondered.

I didn't. But I signed up and got one. Apparently, one can save enough over time to take an early retirement and move to the Bahamas. With that and the coupons I brought along, I saved $11, more than enough to pay for the cranberry juice I drink on the way home as a reward for buying groceries.

But here's the interesting thing—unless you've considered all of this so far to be interesting, in which case "Thank you! Thank you! Oh boy, thank you!"—even with the big savings, my grocery bill was pretty much the same as at the other place.

I am a card-carrying member of the Happy Shopper club now, so I suppose I'll have to go back to the new place sometimes. Still, I'll probably go back to the old place next week.

I think they've learned their lesson by now. Don't you?

UNiDENTiFiED FOODLiKE OBJECTS

Sure, I enjoy buffets. Wanna make something of it?

Now, I know there's a huge anti-buffet contingent out there. The world's full of menu snobs who think buffets are only for those who appreciate overcooked vegetables because they can eat them without putting in their teeth.

But these folks are forgetting the three best things about buffets:

Food.

Food.

And more food.

And all of it, he said in his father's best I-lived-through-the-Depression voice, for one low price!

To completely mangle a Grouchoism, "We lay out a 95-cent buffet that'll knock their eyes out! Course, after we knock their eyes out, we can charge them anything we want!"

So I drag the family to a buffet once in a while, and they go because, well, they're family and they have to. Just like I have to go to the pizza place with the torture tubes and the animatronic band. And waiters.

We all get what we want at a buffet because, deep down in our pleasure centers, what we really want is to eat way too much if we feel like it.

About 15 years ago, I reached the age where I found out the devil's middle name is cholesterol. So at the buffet, I load up on baked chicken, baked fish, and steamed vegetables.

Yeah, I know. The vegetables are overcooked. The carrots and the broccoli are the same color. But you know what? Every once in a while I'll get there at exactly the right moment, when they have just set out the carrots and broccoli, and they still put up a little fight when you bite into them. At that moment it becomes my lucky day, pal, the sun is shining on only me, and I know nothing can go wrong. Those are the times I wish the buffet sold lottery tickets.

My sole nod to the "food I shouldn't eat" group is the peach cobbler. I eat this with a heaping side portion of guilt and spend the rest of the evening telling myself, "Well, you did pretty well foodwise today. Except for the peach cobbler."

My son, meanwhile, gets pizza, fried chicken nuggets, French fries, macaroni and cheese, ice cream, and a peanut butter cookie, in addition to vegetables, which he loves. I dine with him in spirit. My spirit has no cholesterol concerns. My son is as pencil-thin as I was at his age, when I used to sneak a dozen Oreos before dinner.

Sometimes the buffet has entertainment.

Tonight Aaron got a balloon from a guy in a giant bug costume, who I hope and pray worked for the restaurant. And I got to see the most ridiculous toupee on Earth. It was gray and bushy, with a part that showed no scalp, and it teetered atop the old guy's head at a slight tilt, as though one of them was a little tipsy. I only hope he snuck some fish patties out under it so it was useful for something. As hair, it was hopeless.

That's the kind of thing you see at a buffet.

Which brings us to one of the anti-buffet gang's pet peeves: buffet people. That good, honest, salt-substitute-of-the-earth group who will get their money's worth if it keeps 'em up all night going back and forth to the bathroom for Tums. Or just going back and forth to the bathroom.

When I was a kid and we went to the annual summer fair in my little farm town, we always saw people whom we never saw any other time, any other place, as though they existed only that one day a year, and the Troy Free Fair was their *Brigadoon.*

Buffet people strike me that way now.

Look…there are the Darlings, down from the Mayberry hills. And isn't that the Addams Family? And who knew Eb was seeing Bobbie Jo?

The buffet crowd is sort of like the folks who went to church picnics when I was a kid, except none of the buffet people talk to me. So I guess they're exactly like the crowds who went to church picnics when I was a kid.

(The preceding paragraph is a classic example of the Catskill set-up-and-punch gag. Savor it a moment, won't you?)

Personally, I find buffet people encouraging. It's good to see such a large number of folks who have stayed alive for so very, very long. It gives me hope that I may yet one day get to tell my grandchildren to stop flipping spoonfuls of pudding at each other, lest they get us thrown out of the buffet before I finish my tapioca.

So, what can I say with my mouth full? I will always drive half an hour farther down the road to get to the motel with the free breakfast buffet. My wife and I went on a cruise several years ago, and my second-favorite memory is of the buffets. I find limp, soggy green beans comfortable and unassuming.

If the waiter-dependent out there think that makes me as square, tasteless, and old as a buffet fish patty, I can live with that. As long as there's peach cobbler.

BYE, BYE, MISCELLANEOUS PIE

I live in fear of my own heart.

It's not a consuming thing. I don't think about it every morning when I wake up or every night just before I shut the systems down.

But it's there, palpable and palpitating, in my chest.

I was rudely awakened to the fact of my own mortality about 15 years ago. Shortly after moving to Kansas City, I woke up yellow. Not the scared kind. The saffron kind.

I did some checking around and learned that this doesn't automatically happen to everyone who moves to Kansas City. Otherwise, it would be in the song.

"They got some crazy little women there, and I'm gonna turn yellow as a canary…"

I hadn't ordered hepatitis at the fast-food restaurant drive-through just prior to moving north, but it had come with my order anyway.

Part of the treatment included a regular blood test, and the results showed high cholesterol.

Is that a wake-up call I hear?

Obviously it hadn't been my first trip through a fast-food drive-through. My car knew the way by heart. My standard newspaper editor's lunch in those days was a double cheeseburger, fries, and a fried cherry pie. That was after my usual breakfast of coffee and donuts, but before my mid-afternoon candy bar.

Through my childhood, teen years, and my 20s, I assumed that the physical ailments that claimed my father's and grand-father's generation would have no effect on me. The young always think they're bulletproof.

It turns out that being bulletproof and looking good in tights are just two of the things I don't have in common with Superman.

Like many middle-aged guys who learn their cholesterol numbers for the first time, I was scared straight. Oatmeal replaced the donuts. Lunch got lighter, and so did I. "Bippity-boppity-boo!" The candy bar turned into an apple!

As my cholesterol number fell, my fervor dropped off a bit with it. Surely one cookie at work wouldn't hurt. Or two. What was I supposed to do when I was out to dinner, somebody else was buying, and the peach cobbler looked so good? Could I turn down the pork chop my mother had so lovingly fried just for me?

After a while, oatmeal just gets to be so, well, oatmealy.

But then it would come, like a life preserver tossed from a passing ship: a cheap cholesterol screening.

The results would yank me back to reality, like a slap to a panicky guy in a gangster film. My bad cholesterol would again be bad, my good cholesterol would be not so good, and it would be just the goose I needed to become obsessive about my diet again.

This is the cycle I've followed ever since. My theory is that all the ups and downs will even out into a pretty healthy diet.

Of course, the twin mantra of all soldiers in the war on cho-lesterol includes not only diet but also exercise.

I hit the bricks early on. They hit back.

My first experience with jogging had come in my mid-20s. I was out singing folk songs in a bar one night and ran out of breath on a fast song. Next day I laced up bad shoes and went to a park where a one-mile course was laid out.

I have no idea what the far end of that course looks like.

At about the third jog, I began panting like fat Elvis *Live in Hawaii,* and little lightning bolts of pain shot through my side. My calves bawled, and each flat-footed thud sent a shock wave straight up to my teeth.

Jogging became like playing piano—just another thing that looked easy when other people did it. Just another thing I tried briefly before giving up.

Ten years later, after being kicked in the back pockets with that cholesterol number, I tried again. I still wheezed. I still ached. But I kept going. There would be no marathons in my future, but I worked up to a respectable couple of miles a day.

Exercise helped the cholesterol number fall. My spirits rose. It didn't last.

I had become a reader.

Normally I think reading is a good thing. We encourage reading around my house.

The newspapers and magazines I read in those days featured all sorts of experts offering all sorts of advice on keeping that wicked cholesterol number down and putting heart disease in its place, which was not in my chest.

I read, I obeyed, I bored my friends with details and mini-sermons.

Then one day I read the awful word: genetics.

Heart disease, it turns out, has as much to do with heredity as it does with diet or exercise. Or more. Or not as much. It all depends on which expert you read.

I read them all and believed the worst.

My father had his first major heart attack in his 40s. He died way too soon, in his early 60s, from a combination of cancer, diabetes, and heart disease.

Gulp.

So I live in fear of my own heart because it may be the heart of my father.

After reading the stuff about genetics, I could have just surrendered, hung up the jogging shoes, and ordered a big mess of chili fries, I suppose. But I didn't.

If I can't control heredity, I've decided to work a little harder at controlling the other stuff. I may just be kidding myself that it will do any good against genetic predisposition, but, if that's the case, I have myself snookered.

That's why I'm at my company fitness center most days, even though being there reminds me of stalling halfway up the rope in junior high gym.

It's why I regularly humiliate myself in front of guys who have no gray hairs, who can probably do 50 push-ups without breaking a sweat, and who can pee whenever they feel like it.

It's why two lines from a song often go through my head while I work out. The song is not even one I particularly like, but the lines have become a motto.

It's a song off the *End of the Innocence* album by Don Henley, which does have good songs on it, including one of my favorites, "New York Minute." But my two workout lines are from one of the lesser tunes.

"I will not lie down. I will not go quietly."

They inspire me, even though I know they are just a less-poetic version of Dylan Thomas' "Rage, rage against the dying of the light. Do not go gentle into that good night."

It's still Don's two lines that come to mind when the treadmill seems to be going faster than it did last time I ran on it or the weights seem to have gained weight since I last lifted them.

I will not go quietly.

There are too many things I still want to get done to play aces and eights at this stage of the game.

I want to travel with my wife after we both are retired. I want to watch my son graduate from college. I want to figure out all the words to "Green River." I want to sing "Yellow Submarine" to my grandchild.

Get thee behind me, genetics.

I will not lie down.

LET iT OW! LET iT OW! LET iT OW!

I woke up this morning feeling like I'd been beaten with a pillowcase full of cut glass doorknobs.

The places on my body that didn't hurt were places I don't have.

You probably think I'm going to tell you I was sore because I spent the previous day crouching, leaping, and rolling through a back alley on a secret government mission in Constantinople. (I know it's Istanbul now, but to me, it will always be Constantinople.)

I can understand why you'd think that. But not this time. It's worse than that.

It snowed. Not a lot. Not like the fabled snows of my father's childhood, when the tops of the drifts, he later claimed, reached his second-story bedroom window. Enough, though, that I had to shovel the driveway.

There's a five-word phrase I've grown extremely familiar with over the past 10 years or so: "…for a guy my age."

SEE ALSO: "for a guy your age" or "for a guy his age."

Get ready. Here it comes again.

I like to think I've stayed in pretty good shape—wait for it—for a guy my age. I exercise. I take the stairs sometimes. I conquer my lust for chocolate cake with peanut butter icing.

Apparently the muscles you use to shovel snow are muscles

you never use for anything else. Much like that muscle along the underside of your wrist that gets used only when you try to force open a frozen car door.

It didn't seem bad during the actual shoveling. Bitter cold, for sure. I could see my mantra "Holy crap! It's cold!" on the air. Still, after a few minutes I was warmed by the work.

My son was lying on his back on the snow-coated lawn making angels, reminding me of a time when snow was good for something. The sky was a beautiful winter blue, and the flaws in my lawn were hidden by clean, white snow. I was earning that sense of smug suburban superiority that comes from not having the last unshoveled driveway in the cul-de-sac. It wasn't a Norman Rockwell plate, but it wasn't bad.

There were just the slightest hints of what was to come. With each torso twist to shove the shovel under the frozen layer beneath the snow, I felt a little twinge in the handles of love. A shot in my lower back reminded me to lift with my legs. Still, when I finished, I didn't feel too bad. For a guy my age.

Imagine my surprise, then, when I woke up this morning feeling stiff as, well, a stiff.

My lower back and my upper arms were in some sort of competition to see which could ache more. Lifting with my legs had mainly resulted in achy legs. Had I wanted to box with my fate, I wouldn't have been able to make fists to do so.

All in all, just another crick in the neck.

I am occasionally faced these days with these sorts of rude reminders, and I don't appreciate them.

I'll be 50 soon, but inside, where it counts, I'm still 15. It was only yesterday, for heaven's sake, that I could stay up all night and put in a full day of TV the next day with no ill effects. Everything I ate went to my attitude. My ball-and-socket joints had lubrication to spare, and my skin fit like it had been tailor-made for me.

I can bop through life most of the time still convinced that those days are not past. My body's still as young as my spirit. Nothin' is gonna change my world.

Then I shovel the snow off my driveway, and truth comes knocking.

I could surrender and follow the course of good boomer suburbanites everywhere. I could hire the neighbor kid. He's right next door, waiting. I could stand inside my warm living room, sipping hot coffee and staring at him through the narrow window next to our front door.

"Lift with your legs," I'd think. Like that was something he had to worry about.

I could watch until he finished too ridiculously soon, then pay him the money I'd never miss.

But I don't.

Because it's my driveway. And I'm a guy. And I'm not ready.

Do you hear me, aches and pains? I am not ready! Sure, you may impose on my life, uninvited, to remind me of the accumulating pile of days in my past. But you also remind me of something else.

You remind me that everything still works.

Shovel, please.

RHYMES WiTH "OLD"

I am sitting in a little café, eating a burrito the size of my thigh, after having just spent a lovely sunny day people watching.

You'd think I'd be happy, right?

Not completely.

See, I have a cold.

It snuck up on me yesterday while I wasn't paying attention. So technically, it could have been any time yesterday, since I am seldom paying attention. By last night it was in the full flower of coldhood.

Here's something I didn't realize. It turns out that when we humans lie down, a steady pool of stuff flows into our mouths from the back of our throats, and we have to swallow every so often all night long.

It's not something you think about, unless every time you swallow it feels like trying to choke down a sandpaper-coated billiard ball.

I'm surprised the folks in the room next to mine didn't report me for having a dog in my room, since I was barking all night. OK, technically, I was coughing. But it had a definite K-9 lilt.

Stuff was coming out of my nose that had no business being in there in the first place, and I either had a fever, or my hotel bed is over a portal to hell.

So to make a long whine longer, my cold and I got very little sleep.

I have tried to write something every weekday since I started this little project, and so far there's always been a can of something in the old idea cupboard.

Normally spending a day observing will jump-start my muses.

Alas, there was no muse-jumping today. No 60-watt bulb came on directly over my head. "Hallelujah Chorus" never began to play.

See, I did something I never, ever do. I took a cold capsule.

I never take cold capsules because—

A. I'm a guy; and
B. I don't need no stinkin' medicine to handle
   a wimpy little cold because, did I mention,
   I'm a guy?

Technically, of course, women keep going when they have colds too. They just don't whine about it. That and the ability to match socks to dress pants are what separates them from guys.

So I took the cold pills, and I walked around all day feeling like my head was full of oatmeal. Here's a little something I've learned over the years: Belly full of oatmeal, good. Head full of oatmeal, bad.

One of the things I hate most about colds is that a cold makes me feel my age. I read once about a young woman who wanted to write about what it was like to be an old woman. So she had a makeup artist make her look old, then she wore weights and put on clothes that restricted her mobility.

That's what having a cold does to me. And then it doesn't even let me write about it.

The last time I had a cold this bad, I was visiting the FDR memorial in Washington, D.C., and I noticed that the first thing you come to there is a public restroom. I think that's a wonderful tribute. Roosevelt always tried to see to the basic needs of weary, searching people.

There are other reasons FDR is my favorite president. Of course, I wasn't alive when he was in office, but I think he's the best president the country ever had. I don't think it's an exaggeration to say that Roosevelt and Winston Churchill saved the world in the 1940s.

Mostly I admire FDR because he just made sense. His words are eloquent and forceful, yet easily understandable and full of the plain truths that are often so lacking in politics. Lots of good examples are carved on the rocks at his memorial.

One of my favorites:

"I have seen war. I have seen war on land and sea. I have seen blood running from the wounded. I have seen the dead in the mud. I have seen cities destroyed. I have seen children starving. I have seen the agony of mothers and wives. I hate war."

Visitors to FDR's memorial are led through the huge display by his great words until, in the final section, they come upon a statue of FDR in his wheelchair.

It's a controversial addition, of course. Most of the American people never knew FDR was in a wheelchair while he was president. No photograph was published of him in his chair during that time, and the press never printed the fact that he used one.

So, the critics say, Roosevelt would not have wanted to be depicted in a wheelchair in his memorial.

We can never know. But I like to think FDR would have been in favor of anything that showed tourists from around the world that you can accomplish great things in spite of great obstacles.

My visit had special meaning for that day of my cold. It put certain things into perspective for sure. I was reminded that there are far worse things than colds and far better ways to spend your time than whining about having one.

PAPERBACK WRITER, SORT OF

Oh, yeah. Greeting cards and I go way back.

Around the turn of the '60s, my mom and dad would make a weekly five-mile trip into town from the big pink house we lived in. This was when my mom did her shopping for clothes for us kids and mysterious "mom stuff" for herself. My father, meanwhile, waited in the car, smoking. While they were taking care of business, I busied myself at the J.C. Penney.

Sometimes I took the whole time Mom was shopping to decide on the hard plastic Rat Fink or tin cap pistol or *Sad Sack* comic book I was going to spend my allowance on, and I would be begging for additional minutes when she came to get me. Other times, though, I finished in plenty of time to wander over to the greeting card rack.

Once there, I would systematically read every joke card. I was led down the garden path by a promise of cash inside a card that was—and here's the funny part—glued shut! Or I would be tempted with a glimpse at a scantily clad beauty, only to have it turn out to be a chimp. Often the cards talked about martinis, which were about as common in the little town I grew up in as Martians. One card was a long gag on a card that opened to be several cards tall, and the end was a pun.

"Who was that masked man?"

"That was…the Lone Arranger!"

Puns were my favorite form of humor then, and if you haven't given up reading and turned on the TV by this point, you know they still are.

I always got a few laughs at the greeting card rack.

A few years later, I actually had occasion to buy cards.

Girls became suddenly interesting, and in the frantic, lifelong search for a way to make them like me as desperately as I liked them, I turned to greeting cards.

Peanuts cards, to be exact.

People are fans of Peanuts now, but they forget how fanatic we were about them in the mid-'60s. Charlie Brown and his friends were every bit as pervasive a cultural phenomenon as James Bond, *Laugh-In,* the Twist, or yo-yos.

I sent them exclusively. Linus was my favorite. His good, tolerant, open nature in the sneering face of life was nothing short of inspirational. In a different format, he was preaching the same "All You Need Is Love" message as the Beatles. And in the era of Vietnam and ever-impending nuclear annihilation, we needed that.

The cards I sent to girls in far-off Pennsylvania towns probably paid for a lot of Charles Schulz's pens, and for that I am most pleased.

A few years later it dawned on me that I could just write my own greeting cards. I could make up bad puns just as well as the next person with a pencil and a thesaurus.

In college I sent one to a girl I was wooing, in the hopes of woo-hooing. It was the early 1970s, and profanity was as much a part of our conversation as verbs. This particular card was a long way from Lucy and Schroeder at the piano.

COVER: "Elizabeth Barrett Browning once wrote: 'How do I love thee? Let me count the ways? I love thee to the depth and breadth and height my soul can reach, when feeling out of sight for the ends of being and ideal grace…'"
INSIDE: "Poetic little mother, wasn't she?"

Except it didn't say "mother."

The girl I sent it to later told me she laughed so hard she had to sit down, which was pretty much what I intended.

It never occurred to me that I could write greeting cards for a living. For one thing, I thought my style of humor—if it could be called that—was all wrong. I was way too *Smothers Brothers Comedy Hour* and not nearly enough *Brady Bunch*. And then there was the big bugaboo: I can't draw. I mean, I really can't draw. I can't draw a straight line with a ruler. My stick figures turn out fat.

I knew for sure that the same people who wrote the cards drew them. What company would be cool enough to pay a person just to write greeting card gags all day?

That wasn't a job. I knew what a job was. A job was my dad going out in the dead of winter in an old cloth coat to climb telephone poles in the bitter wind to repair frozen lines. A job was my uncle starting to throw rough, heavy bales onto a wagon at dawn and still hefting them after dark. Those were jobs.

Why do you think I was so desperate to be a musician?

Some time later I was the editor of a small-town newspaper, and part of my job was to write a humor column twice each week. It doesn't take long to scrape the bottom of the idea barrel at that rate. Soon you're checking to see if the barrel has a false bottom and maybe there are some secret ideas stashed underneath.

Our wedding anniversary came around, and my wife sent me a card.

COVER: "I love you more today than yesterday."
INSIDE: "Yesterday, you really got on my nerves."

This time it was my turn to laugh so hard I had to sit down.

The card was perfect for us, as though the writer had been spying on our marriage when we weren't looking. Plus, it was funnier than Ernie Kovacs on one of his hot nights. I was so impressed, I wrote a column about it.

It was fine being a newspaper editor, except for one thing. The newspaper business doesn't have much respect for creativity, which puts it pretty much in line with the rest of American society. To move up the ladder in the newspaper game, you really have to move away from writing and toward management. And if I couldn't sing for a living, I wanted to write.

I saw in a magazine ad that a greeting card company calling itself "SHOEBOX (A Tiny Little Division of Hallmark)" was seeking writers.

The anniversary card had been a Shoebox.

When I was a kid, the joke page of *Boy's Life* magazine offered to pay a fortune—five bucks—for any joke a scout sent in that they published. I sent in every joke I knew—about 100—laboriously written on a Big Chief tablet in pencil. I had spent the money in my head a dozen times over by the time I heard back. They weren't going to buy any of them.

I was thinking about that as I sent in the 10 card ideas Shoebox requested as an application, including a sanitized version of the Elizabeth Barrett Browning card and a pun involving a fish that called itself a "greeting cod."

I was so sure they wouldn't like my ideas I didn't even tell my wife I had applied, so she was just as surprised as I was when the call came for an interview.

I will try to say this next part as humbly as I can. Up to that point I had always been the funniest guy in the room. I'd read or seen funnier people on TV or in movies, but I had never met anyone funnier than I was.

Until my Shoebox interview dinner. I sat with Steve, the writing manager for Shoebox at the time, and Dan, one of the writers, and tried to keep afloat in the sea of banter. I felt like I'd worn the cement shoes.

To make a long story end before you run screaming from the room, I got the job.

My first day, after spending the entire morning doing necessary paperwork, they told me not to feel like I had to actually write any cards that afternoon.

Right. Like that was the hard part.

At Shoebox in those days the staff of nine writers wrote card ideas all day, on three-by-five index cards folded in half, each scribe Catskilled away in his or her tiny cubicle. Then, at four, all the writers slumped and shuffled into a tiny room and sat around a table. Steve read each idea aloud and said on the spot which ones were good enough to be tested as Shoebox cards and which weren't.

And if the maiden tied to the chair wasn't drowned when the village elders pulled her out of the river, she wasn't a witch.

The cards that were routinely being turned down my first day were funnier than anything I'd written. All of my pearls were heading for the reject box as well.

On the other hand, this little room full of the funniest people I'd ever met were laughing at some of my ideas. A dog in a classroom of first graders couldn't get strokes as positive as that.

Then I got an idea accepted. Then another.

Suddenly, I felt a little less like Harpo at the Algonquin.

It's been more than 15 years now, and I'm still at it. Several thousand "It's your birthday!" jokes later, I still love getting that assignment in the morning and writing those cards all day. It feels like an old corduroy suit coat.

This will always be the job that made me forget about music. It's the only job I've ever had that I hope they let me keep until I retire.

I consider myself the luckiest class clown in Kansas City. And that includes both the Kansas and Missouri sides.

DUDE, WHERE'S MY FLYING CAR?

One of the best things about writing Shoebox and Hallmark cards all these years has been writing for Maxine.

Maxine isn't a person. Not a real one, anyway, unless you live in a world where Homer Simpson and Linus Van Pelt are real people. And if you do, can I come visit you sometime?

Maxine is the old lady on those old lady cards. She's the one with the blue hair, the keen powers of observation, and the acidic wit.

She is the one who says the things we think of the next day and wish we'd said. She takes no prisoners, which is just as well. One wonders what she would do with prisoners once she had some.

For years she's been one of the most popular characters on Shoebox greeting cards, so a few years ago we decided to put her in a syndicated comic strip. Rather than wisecrack her usual greeting card jokes about how old somebody was getting, Maxine now had the chance to wax crabby on news events of the day.

Once this happened, the writers began hearing news and current events in a different way. Suddenly, in addition to thinking "Well, that was interesting!" we began to think "What would that wacky Maxine make of this?"

We don't write the daily comic strip anymore, but I still find myself thinking of Maxine lines when I hear some interesting bit of news.

Today I heard a piece of news that begs for a Maxine joke.

There's a supermarket in California that lets customers charge stuff without credit cards, by using a fingerprint scanner. Apparently, shoppers can just have their fingerprints put online, then touch an electronic reader when it comes time to pay the grocer.

And Maxine says, "Usually when I give a supermarket the finger, it's because they shorted the foot-long wieners."

Or, the one we wouldn't have been able to do, "So I guess now instead of trying to rip off my credit cards, the crooks will just rip off my finger."

Yep. Stuff like that is what I get paid for. Quite a world we live in.

Unlike Maxine, my first response on hearing the fingerprint story was fairly positive. "All right!" I thought, "Now we're getting someplace!"

For most of our lives, we've been assured that cool inventions were just around the corner. Turns out to be a great big corner, difficult to circumvent.

If you don't believe me, just hop in your flying car and come on down and we'll talk about it.

Oh, wait. You don't have a flying car, do you?

OK, then, call me on your wristwatch TV screen.

Oh, yeah. You don't have a wristwatch TV screen.

It's actually just as well that you don't try to contact me. I'll be vacationing at my summer place on the moon.

Oh, wait…

Where's the far-out stuff we were promised?

That strip down the highway that autopilots your car so you can spend the whole trip from Pennsylvania to Kansas learning to play harmonica? I want that!

The computer that reads your mind and writes what you think, spelled correctly and full of words you don't actually know? I want that!

The car that runs on water? Bring it on!

The pill that makes you irresistible to the opposite sex? Well, actually, I don't need that one…

Sure, we have some cool inventions. Food courts, for example, like the one I'm sitting in right now, typing on a laptop computer. Oh yeah, and laptop computers.

I have a friend who looks up a Swedish newspaper every morning on his hand-held computer. That's pretty neat.

I was embarrassed in the second grade because I couldn't tie my sneaks. My son has Velcro.

And I still don't believe that microwave ovens work. I use one, but I still can't believe it. That's as close to Buck Rogers as we've gotten. And I'm talking the good Buck Rogers from movie serials, not the dumb TV series one.

Not only don't we have a lot of the cool stuff we were supposed to have, a lot of the inventions we do have are of questionable value.

I heard the fingerprint story at the fitness center. They've installed TVs in front of the treadmill. One of them plays CNN, the other plays ESPN. To hear them, you have to wear one of those radios on your head. I have yet to find one that feels comfortable on my head or in my ears.

Actually, nothing feels comfortable in my ears. And even hair isn't comfortable on my head.

So I don't listen. But I can't stop watching. If there's a TV playing, I must watch. It's hardwired into my circuitry. So that's how I caught the fingerprint story, by reading a crawl across the bottom of a TV screen while running on a treadmill.

Meanwhile, a radio was playing modern rock, which I must listen to because it beats putting something uncomfortable in my ears.

OK, we can do all this stuff. We have the technology. We can put a TV in every building in America and fill all silence with music.

Big whoop. Where are my x-ray glasses?

I just got used to automatic flush toilets, then they sprang automatic sink faucets on me. Now they have a bathroom faucet that comes on automatically behind your back as soon as the auto-flush urinal kicks in. I'm thinking the only thing left is an automatic fly-zipper. I'm not sure if I'm excited about that or not.

OK, so I'm a little excited about it.

I don't like CDs either. Go ahead and spout on about how great they are, how much information they hold, how inde-structible they are. To me they're still just Capri pants.

See, I think Capri pants were thought up by designers who wanted to embarrass women into replacing their perfectly good blue jeans. Blue jeans just don't wear out fast enough, so they must be made obsolete by designers. Women must be made to feel inadequate if their pants go four inches too far down their legs.

In the same way, I still believe CDs are part of a larger plot to force me to replace my entire cassette tape collection at 20 bucks a pop album. And just never you mind that I still have actual albums and a record player for them in my basement.

If you added up all the great inventions that haven't been invented yet and all the lame ones that have, well…you'd have to be better with big numbers than I am.

If only there was some sort of hand-held electronic device that did math problems…

iT'S ONLY WORDS

If you're still with me after all these words, you and I probably share the same wish by now.

We both wish I were a great writer.

Sorry.

I know great writers. I have read great writers. I, sir, am no great writer.

I'm at the age now where it would be nice to be great at something. There's plenty of space on the mantel where an Olympic Gold Medal would fit nicely, or a Grammy, or a Pulitzer Prize. The only differences between me and the people who have those things are natural talent, luck, and hard work. That's why they're great.

Instead, I'm about average at a lot of things and a little above average at a couple of things. I just never wanted to work hard enough to become great at anything.

Writing has always been fun. To become a whole lot better at it would have meant turning it into hard work. No thanks. I have plenty of things in my life that are hard work.

I've been a writer almost since I learned how to write. If all the words I've written over the years were laid end to end, they would make one great big word that didn't make any sense.

From crayons to pencils to pens to an Underwood typewriter as heavy as a horse, right on through to word processors, computers, and this laptop, I've spent the better part of a lifetime lining up words.

In sixth grade we had a limerick contest. Our assignment was to write a limerick about our principal, Mr. Webster. Most of the kids wore their Number 2s to nubs trying to rhyme with "Webster." Twice.

My audacious and disrespectful solution to the problem was to rhyme with Mr. Webster's first name, Frank.

Much easier.

Here it is:

> My teacher's name is Frank.
> He drives to school in a tank.
> He teaches school
> And the Golden Rule
> And he keeps all his money in a bank.

There's a reason I remember that limerick, word for word, 40 years later. It's because when Mr. Webster read my limerick aloud, the whole class laughed.

That laughter was better than recess, better than chocolate pinwheel cookies, better than Saturday morning television.

And it's one of the reasons I write for a living now. It's one of the reasons I would be a writer even if I didn't get paid for it. It's one of the reasons I'm writing this paragraph.

When you're shorter than the other boys, and not good at sports, and not brilliant or handsome or particularly popular, a laugh is a priceless gift.

As I hammer out these essays, I keep thinking about what a strange thing it is to want to write. Who do I think I am that anyone should give a rat's underpants about what I think? Do I really suppose I'll make a difference? Do I think this pile of words will amount to a hill of beans?

No, I don't.

Maybe if I were a great writer…

I write because nobody has stopped me yet and because Hallmark pays me to do it and, most of all, because it's still fun.

I used to think it was vital that I left something behind. I felt an urgency to be certain that I would be remembered after I had joined Clarence and earned my wings.

Somewhere along the path, that notion fell out of my pack. Nowadays I think spending so much time trying to become a little bit immortal keeps a person from living in the day. And I like the day.

It would be nice if someone read these pages one day. It would be nice if he or she laughed. It would be nice if the "you" I keep referring to wasn't just the other me. But if I knew nobody would ever read them, I'd write them anyway.

Did I mention it's fun?

While I was stomping the treadmill today, I watched college-level women's fast-pitch softball on ESPN. The women played determined and hard because they wanted to win.

I doubt that any of them will sign million-dollar contracts with the majors, or make millions more shilling cereal, or get second and third chances if they're caught with drugs.

I went to a few women's softball games when I lived in Washington and saw firsthand that they play for the love of the game. You can actually feel it when you watch them play.

That's why I keep writing—to feel the love of the game.

I wrote my first book when I was eight or nine. It was about a 10-foot-tall alien who crash-landed on Earth and made friends with a little boy named Billy. The alien's crashed spaceship was called "Starduster," which was also the name of the spaceship on a cartoon show I used to watch.

It's probably not a coincidence that my elementary class had just finished reading a book about an alien who crash-landed on Earth and made friends with a little boy. But the difference—and this is key—was that the alien in that book was three feet tall.

So my work was, of course, totally original.

I remembered my book as I was videotaping my son reading his first book to his first-grade class. Everyone in the class had been assigned to write and illustrate a book. This was a special reading for parents.

My son's book was *Super Diaper Dog,* about a superhero dog that defeats a villainous, jewel-thieving cat. There is a section in the narrative where Super Diaper Dog is warned to watch out because "That cat knows kung fu!" Aaron read it with the appropriate gusto.

His classmates laughed.

If a person could smile so wide that it would reach clear around to the back of his head, I would have.

I was every bit as proud and delighted as every other parent in the room when his or her kid read. But along with the pride and pleasure, I felt something else…

I really wanted to write about it.

YOU SAY IT'S MY BIRTHDAY

COVER: You're proof positive that the fun doesn't have to end at 50!
INSIDE: No, the fun has to end at 7:30.

*   *   *   *   *

COVER: I can't be 50!
INSIDE: I still like rock and roll!

*   *   *   *   *

COVER: You're 50! You know what that means?
INSIDE: The distance you had to walk to school in the snow just doubled.

*   *   *   *   *

COVER: You're 50!
INSIDE: Tell us again how good rock and roll used to be before those corporate bean counters got hold of it, won't you?

*   *   *   *   *

COVER: You're 50!
INSIDE: 'bout time to start writing rambling letters to the editor signed "Just a Citizen," isn't it?

*   *   *   *   *

COVER: Now that you're 50, the age of skintight jeans is behind you.

INSIDE: For that matter, the age of skintight skin is behind you.

*   *   *   *   *

COVER: Birthdays are like a 50-year-old's sex life.

INSIDE: Once a year, you get something nice.

*   *   *   *   *

Those are a few of the Shoebox cards I've written mocking 50-year-olds over the years. I guess now the comfortable shoe is on the other wrinkly, hair-covered foot.

When I wrote those cards for 50-year-olds, I was using standard age-slam myths, which are exaggerated by greeting card writers for humorous effect.

To wit: Old people sleep all the time. Old people don't dress fashionably. Old people tell long, rambling stories about their younger days.

Guess what? They're true.

I often do go to bed before 10 p.m. This is because, after carefully considering all options, getting a good night's sleep is the most attractive one.

I really do still like rock and roll, just like most people my age, and I really do think it's been ruined by people who mass-produce pap for profit.

My son really is subjected to stories of how he should be grateful for all of his toys because I had to pretend sticks were six-guns.

I really do have wrinkles. I really do have stray hairs in odd places. I really do make a lowland gorilla grunt when I bend over to pick up the morning paper.

That old guy I've been making sport of for 15 years? Turns out it's me.

Some folks think you shouldn't make fun of 50-year-olds. These are people who wear beige all the time and mow their lawns in that waffle crosscut pattern. Pay them no mind.

Many things about me may decline with age, but my sense of humor isn't one of them. I dread the birthday when people stop making fun of me because that will be the day when I know they have started feeling sorry for me.

I don't want your pity. I want a few laughs.

Start getting those 60-year-old jokes ready now.

I know those are some of my "You're 50!" cards because Allyson printed them out and brought them to my birthday lunch. Allyson is also a Hallmark card writer, and she could have brought pages of cards she's written that were as funny as any of mine.

Instead, her attached note said she decided to mock me in my own words.

I think it says something about my job that the folks I wanted to share my birthday lunch with are writers and artists I work with. Some of the people around the lunch table were at Shoebox when I got there 15 years ago. A couple of others came shortly after. These are friendships that have simmered a long time.

While I don't think we'll ever do a group hug and break into "A Long Way to Tipperary," I do cherish those people.

Besides, I figured people were bound to mock me on my birthday, and I wanted the mocking done by professionals who are good at it. They did not let me down.

Plus, they paid for my pancakes and brought me a great history-nerd book about the Civil War.

Fifty rocks!

*   *   *   *   *

As we ate and talked, the gang around the table was staring at my forehead, all of them too polite to mention the red scab glowing like Rudolph's nose.

Finally I just told them. I was at my in-laws' house for Father's Day, and I walked into a low-hanging planter.

This little wound, clearly visible where hair used to be, has had an unfortunate effect.

From the time my father lost his hair, it seemed like there was always a bruise atop his head in some stage of healing. He got most of those gashes while doing home repair projects, which he loved to do.

So when I looked in the mirror and saw the crimson mark on my head, I saw my father staring back at me. And not my young father, the one I remember from when I was a boy. The older, balder one.

Usually this only happens when I whistle. My dad was a great whistler. Recently I was absentmindedly whistling, when I looked in a mirror and, except for the beard, there was my father's face whistling back.

I don't know much about relativity, but I know your father is always older than you are. My dad's gone now, and suddenly I'm catching up. This will take some getting used to, and my 50th birthday isn't the best day for it.

I head-butted the planter twice during that visit to my in-laws. I often whack my head on the low tree branch while mowing the lawn or the car doorframe while reaching across the seat. I usually have a bruise showing through sparse hair cover. Like Les Nessman, you never know where my latest Band-

Aid will be.

Great. I had to inherit that…couldn't get the talent for whistling…oh no…that would be asking too much…

*   *   *   *   *

Like many days you anticipate in life, my 50th birthday was kind of an anti-climax.

Make your 50-year-old guy joke here.

Certainly, there were high points.

The day started with a big, shiny "You're 50!" balloon and a birthday cake, one of which we ate for breakfast.

And, of course, my wife and I went someplace special and romantic for dinner; assuming you consider the middle of the woods surrounded by Cub Scouts special and romantic.

My birthday fell during Scout Day-Camp Week, and the actual day was parents' night at the camp. Like our pioneer ancestors, we bought subs and chips and forged a trail to the campsite. I ate my turkey with fat-free honey mustard while sitting on the sub wrapper, tilting backwards downhill in the dirt, listening to sweaty, mud-encrusted, laughing seven-year-old boys telling us about the day at camp.

If I have to tell you that I loved it, then you haven't been paying attention.

Once past our repast, we followed the boys down a narrow, jagged trail through the woods, even though all the moms were wearing sandals. At the end of the path, we stood on a ledge that looked out over a river, nervous when the boys got too close to a wire strung a good five feet from the edge. On the way back, my wife found a tick on her sleeve. There were signs along the trail identifying leaves, and I leaned in close to read one: "Poison Ivy."

Back at home, while Aaron showered off the topsoil he'd

brought home on his person, I took the dog out for his nightly sniff-n-spray.

I often talk to myself while walking the dog, and this night I tried out different inflections to use when I told people I was 50.

There was the "I know! I can't believe it either!" tone of voice. Then I tried the "Oh, I'm 50, but it doesn't really mean anything" inflection. There was the "bummer, man" kind of a resigned-to-the-awful-truth tone. There was the self-mocking "just call me geezer" laugh.

None of them sounded quite correct. Fortunately I walk the dog every night and will have lots of time to get it right before I turn 51.

After that it was quarter to 10, and since a 50th birthday only comes once in a lifetime, I decided to spend the rest of mine doing something I would really enjoy.

I went to sleep for the night.

*   *   *   *   *

So after several months of writing and reflecting about turning 50, I think I'm finally ready to answer the question, "What does all of this mean?"

And here's the answer:

I dunno.

But I've found myself thinking about two words from my favorite novel quite a bit over the past several days.

"Thou mayest."

In John Steinbeck's *East of Eden,* two characters have a debate over two words in the Old Testament. The debate centers over whether a Hebrew word should be translated "Thou shalt" or "Thou mayest."

I've been spending a lot of time lately worrying about "can" and "can't" and "able" and "unable." Will I still be able at 50 to do all the things I could do at 30?

Maybe that's the wrong question.

A better question might be "Do I still want to do all the things I could do at 30, even if I can?"

Or am I old enough now to know that life isn't a contest that you have to win but a celebration you can choose to enjoy?

If the first two-thirds of my life were spent trying to do all that I could, maybe the last third might be better spent choosing to do things that I know are important and right.

Too much of my past, I suspect, was spent worrying about things that didn't really matter and chasing things I didn't really need, while the important things were right in front of my eyes the whole time.

Family. Friends. Love.

Health. Home. Faith.

Life.

I think part of my inability to answer the big "What's it all about?" question is that I'm just not ready yet. I don't know enough. Perhaps I never will.

So in that unique way that boomers have of avoiding the difficult, I'm leaning toward replacing that one with a different question too.

What's next?

We made love, not war; gave peace a chance; tuned in, turned on, and dropped out; and shook our groove thang.

Now what? I don't know the answer to that question, either. But I'm excited about finding it.

AND IN THE END...

So after 50 years, here's what I think I've learned:
1. Most people mean well, so everyone deserves the benefit of the doubt.
2. Love is always worth the effort.
3. Life is good.

ABOUT THE AUTHOR

Bill Gray is a humor writer, musician, and baby boomer who has made his way to 50-something with a soundtrack playing in his mind. It's the sound of a dozen garage bands; the sound of revolution meeting middle age; and always, always the sound of four guys from Liverpool whom he never met.

When he isn't writing humor cards for Hallmark, Bill loves being with his wife, Carolyn, and son, Aaron, at their home in Shawnee, Kansas, where sometimes he plays guitar, sometimes he plays drums, and sometimes he just plays.

iF YOU HAVE ENJOYED THiS BOOK

or it has touched your life in some way,
Hallmark would love to hear from you.

BOOK FEEDBACK

2501 McGee, Mail Drop 250
Kansas City, MO 64141-6580
Or e-mail us at booknotes@hallmark.com